THE SURVIVAL GUIDE

100 DAYS TO CONQUER YOUR FEARS, SHATTER YOUR LIMITS, AND BUILD YOUR FAITH

JUSTIN STUART AND ANDREW SCITES

WITH JOSHUA COOLEY

ILLUSTRATIONS BY STEVE WACKSMAN

Tommy NELSON®

An Imprint of Thomas Nelson

The JStu Survival Guide: 100 Days to Conquer Your Fears, Shatter Your Limits, and Build Your Faith

© 2024 Justin Stuart and Andrew Scites

Tommy Nelson, PO Box 141000, Nashville, TN 37214

Published in Nashville, Tennessee, by Tommy Nelson. Tommy Nelson is an imprint of Thomas Nelson. Thomas Nelson is a registered trademark of HarperCollins Christian Publishing, Inc.

Tommy Nelson titles may be purchased in bulk for educational, business, fundraising, or sales promotional use. For information, please e-mail SpecialMarkets@ThomasNelson.com.

Unless otherwise noted, Scripture quotations taken from the ESV® Bible (The Holy Bible, English Standard Version®). Copyright © 2001 by Crossway, a publishing ministry of Good News Publishers. Used by permission. All rights reserved.

Scripture quotations marked NCV are taken from the New Century Version®. Copyright © 2005 by Thomas Nelson. Used by permission. All rights reserved.

Scripture quotations marked NIV are taken from The Holy Bible, New International Version®, NIV®. Copyright © 1973, 1978, 1984, 2011 by Biblica, Inc.® Used by permission of Zondervan. All rights reserved worldwide. www.Zondervan.com. The "NIV" and "New International Version" are trademarks registered in the United States Patent and Trademark Office by Biblica, Inc.®

Scripture quotations marked NLT are taken from the Holy Bible, New Living Translation. © 1996, 2004, 2015 by Tyndale House Foundation. Used by permission of Tyndale House Ministries Carol Stream, Illinois 60188. All rights reserved.

ISBN 978-1-4002-5047-9 (audiobook)
ISBN 978-1-4002-5048-6 (eBook)
ISBN 978-1-4002-5043-1 (HC)

Library of Congress Cataloging-in-Publication Data

LCCN 2024018607

Written by Justin Stuart and Andrew Scites with Joshua Cooley

Illustrated by Steve Wacksman

Printed in Canada

24 25 26 27 28   TC   10 9 8 7 6 5 4 3 2

Mfr: TC Transcontinental / Beauceville, Canada / October 2024 / PO #12291719

CONTENTS

HELLO!

I'm Justin
I'm Andrew.
And we are JStu!

We grew up as next-door neighbors, and we loved making videos together. We would film all kinds of random ideas on Andrew's camcorder. Then came along this new website called YouTube. We started uploading our silly recordings for friends and family to enjoy, and our channel just grew and grew and grew. Cool!

On the JStu channel, the sole mission of our videos is to help people laugh daily. We want to make life brighter, funnier, and a little more ridiculous for all of you. And as we do that, we get to travel the globe, build incredible things, and grow a fun business alongside a talented, super-awesome team. Double cool!

Through budget challenges, fort building, dares, and dangers, we've done more than just have fun (and we survived—whew!). We've learned a ton of deeper lessons about God along the way. It's amazing what you can learn from a leaky submarine, a night spent on the face of a cliff, a warehouse full of toilet paper, or a staple gun accident. We've had a lot of crazy experiences—good and bad—but Jesus has remained the same.

Now years later (in fact, two wives, six kids, three dogs, a cat, a dozen chickens, and a few ducks later), we made a BOOK! Inside, you'll find a bunch of life lessons we've learned through our crazy adventures. Our goal is to point to the truths God has revealed to us through our experiences and to encourage you to seek after a relationship with the Creator of everything: Jesus! You are going to learn a lot about who God is and how much He cares about YOU.

Some devotionals are thirty days long or sixty days long. Some are even ninety days. But *The JStu Survival Guide* is one hundred awesome, adventure-filled days long! So now it's our turn to challenge *you*! Journey through this book, and ask God to show you something really cool. And BONUS! In each section, you'll find an epic, JStu-style challenge. Check with an adult, gather supplies, and get ready to be a boss!

Are you ready? Complete this 100-day challenge, and you will walk away with a new perspective that will radically shift how you experience life. And we very much hope it inspires you to go all out for Jesus!

Enjoy the ride!

—JUSTIN AND ANDREW

THE ULTIMATE MAKER

In the beginning, God created the heavens and the earth.
—GENESIS 1:1

Our journey in life includes some epic moments: our shaky first steps, the first time we score in a game, the scary leap into a first job. These moments and so many others are the hidden building blocks of our lives, creating our story piece by piece.

I remember one of these important moments pretty well. When I was young, my parents gave me my first video camera (long before we had cameras on our phones!). Suddenly I felt like I had become a famous movie director—the Steven Spielberg of my own living room.

Before long, I had produced an overload of home movies. And trust me, they'll never see the light of day! The simple joy of seeing myself on-screen eclipsed any concerns about my charisma on video or the opinions of others. I was in my zone—just creating, unaware of the world's judgments. It felt like an artist had been trapped inside me, trying to burst out, and the video camera finally gave me the canvas I could paint on.

Little did I know, this playful season would snowball into creating our very own YouTube channel. Talk about an unexpected plot twist! I never envisioned my love for video-making evolving into a full-blown career, but God had a bigger plan in mind.

My personal creative journey causes me to reflect on God, the original Creator who has been at work since before time began. My transformation from a kid with a camera to a video-making career wasn't just by chance; my all-powerful Creator had drawn up a perfect plan for me.

My journey shows how God can shape each of us with a unique purpose. He doesn't make mistakes—ever. Your life is not an accident. It's a masterpiece mapped out by the Creator—regardless of who you are, what you look like, or what you're interested in.

So lean into the wild adventure of life, and trust your Creator. The One who crafted the galaxies isn't a distant force. He intricately designed you and wants a relationship with you. So explore the person God created you to be, embrace the chaos, and in the meantime, enjoy this fact: the same Creator who made the universe is painting a masterpiece in you.

— JUSTIN

TREEHOUSE VIEW

O LORD, our Lord, how majestic is your name in all the earth! You have set your glory above the heavens.

—PSALM 8:1

Have you ever watched a sunset and gotten lost in the explosion of colors in the sky? I sure have, especially when we slept overnight in the world's most luxurious treehouse.

In 2022, the JStu crew was invited to spend the night in an incredible "treehouse" (a super-cool vacation rental) in Bailey, Colorado, right in the middle of the Rocky Mountains. At the time, the treehouse was valued at more than $1.6 million! It was an amazing experience.

Inside, the treehouse had everything we needed. We even enjoyed a scrumptious meal cooked by a five-star chef! And in the bathroom, we got our first experience with a bidet, complete with a remote control. (Don't know what a bidet is? Google it and you'll be "flush" with info.)

But as cool as the inside of the treehouse was, the views from the deck were mind-blowing! I could see for miles in every direction. It was as if I had stepped into a dream. All around us, the ground was carpeted with lush, green pines. Mountains rose majestically in the distance. And the sky was so blue it looked like it had been Photoshopped. We were surrounded by the grandeur of creation.

That experience reminds me of something far bigger and more magnificent than a five-star treehouse: God's glory. You may be thinking, *Um, Justin, what is that exactly?* I like to think of God's glory as noticing what makes Him so different from us humans, like seeing His creativity and power on display. I often see His glory best when I stop and look at the incredible things He's made.

Taking a moment to soak in God's incredible creation is like hitting pause on life. Whether it's watching an insane sunset, listening to a beautiful symphony of birds in the trees, or even peering down at a little bug doing its thing on a leaf, there's wonder waiting around every corner. All you have to do is open your eyes and look for it. So get out there and find some of that God-made awesomeness today.

— JUSTIN

UNLOCK YOUR CREATIVITY

O LORD, what a variety of things you have made! In wisdom you have made them all.

—PSALM 104:24 NLT

God is amazingly creative. His imagination is boundless. And you know what's crazy? He has the power to bring all His genius ideas to life!

As you look around outside, just think of the variety of things God has made, from bark on the trees to clouds in the sky to worms in the dirt. And everything in creation has a purpose. God intentionally made each plant, animal, bird, and bug.

I love looking at the stars and getting lost in thought. I think about how beautiful the night sky looks, filled with twinkling star-light, and how huge the universe is. God created day and night, but He didn't leave the night pitch-black; He gave us little night-lights in the darkness!

Remarkably, this same infinitely creative God who invented the stars has crafted you and me. He made us in His image and made us to be creative as well! For Justin and me, our creative impulses result in online videos. We've been making YouTube videos for about thirteen years now, and our work requires us to constantly be imaginative and resourceful.

People often ask me, "How do you guys stay creative?" Simply put, we lean on God for inspiration. He guides us when we're at

a loss for ideas—even when we're really in the zone and the ideas are overflowing.

One of the most creative video series we do is our budget challenges. This is where everyone in the video is given a different amount of money to accomplish the same goal—often to build a structure to spend the night in.

In one video, the goal was to build survival structures using only items from Hobby Lobby. Now, Hobby Lobby wouldn't be my first choice for finding what we need to build outdoor survival forts, but that's where the creativity comes in! Whether a team member has the lowest budget of $100 or the highest budget of $1,000, we have to be creative in how we build a fort with random store-bought items.

Your creativity might not involve forts, survival gear, or large retail chains. But God has gifted you with unique skills and creativity. Because God is creative, you are too! He made you in His image, providing you with different abilities, interests, and creative instincts. You just need to find where you thrive.

Putting yourself in situations that require imagination, originality, and resourcefulness helps stimulate the creativity inside you. You can think outside the box because you were made by a God who thinks that way too. So find out what you're good at, and let God's creativity flow through you!

—ANDREW

READ THIS DEVOTION OUTSIDE AND REFLECT ON GOD'S AMAZING CREATIVITY!

POWER STATION

I know that you can do anything,
and no one can stop you.
—JOB 42:2 NLT

Have you ever hit the gym or busted out some intense physical activity only to wake up the next day feeling like you were hit by a truck? Been there, done that.

Not long ago, I played a game of flag football. No big deal, right? I thought I was in peak shape. But reality hit hard the next morning. I felt like I'd crossed into a parallel universe where the freedom to move body parts without pain was a luxury. My muscles were staging a rebellion. What a humbling experience!

Those slightly embarrassing moments of human weakness make me ponder the infinite abilities and power of God. Think about it: God never clocks out. He's always at work, keeping the universe running. And it's *easy* for Him! God never pulls a hammy, tweaks an ankle, wakes up sore, or needs some time in the hot tub.

So the next time you're facing a tough decision or difficult situation, remember this: God is powerful. And He has the ability to do everything in His will.

Kind of changes your perspective on things, doesn't it? Waves may crash over your life, and today may throw curveballs, but God remains unshaken. He always finishes His to-do list to perfection.

This confidence in God's ability helped a Bible character named Job weather some of the worst trials ever. In a blink, Job lost all his children, his stuff, and even his health (Job 1–2). Yet when Job considered God's power, Job found the hope and strength to keep going. "I know that you can do anything," he said, "and no one can stop you." Eventually the storm of hardship passed, and God powerfully restored Job's health, family, and prosperity.

You might feel like a total lightweight, but when you trust in the Lord, you're hitching your wagon to the God who effortlessly holds everything together. He doesn't even break a sweat managing galaxies—so handling your stuff is a piece of cake for Him.

In your moments of weakness, you can tap into the perfect strength of a God who doesn't just have *some* power—He has *all* power! He defines *power.* Your uncertainties and challenges are in the hands of the One who doesn't flinch at the chaos.

When adversity strikes, stand tall knowing that the God who has all power is on your side.

— JUSTIN

GOD DOESN'T FLINCH AT CHAOS.

ATTENTION: MASTER PLANNER AT WORK

**Great is our Lord, and abundant in power;
his understanding is beyond measure.**
—PSALM 147:5

One of our most difficult videos involved trapping our buddy Isaac inside a tent for a whopping seven days in the cold Colorado winter. The catch? He would earn $10,000 if he braved the entire time without leaving the tent. Crazy, right?

As we filmed, we created daily challenges and threw a few curveballs—and literal snowballs!—at Isaac. We kept him guessing with surprises around every corner. But the whole time we planned to see him come out victorious and win the big prize. Only he didn't know that!

This crazy video reminds me of what happens when we live with God's perfect wisdom and knowledge. Just like Isaac was in the dark in the tent challenge, we're often unaware of what's around the corner for *us*. Life can be filled with stress, challenges, and the unknown. Sometimes we forget that God is the ultimate Master Planner. And no matter what trials hit us, He is preparing good things for us.

God isn't trivial or malicious. He doesn't toy with us like we did

18

with Isaac during the tent challenge. In fact, God works *everything* in our lives together for good (Romans 8:28). Even when we're confused or scared about the future, we can trust Him. And here's the good news: that means we can live in peace and freedom!

Perhaps you're struggling with uncertainties today. Maybe the future feels scary. Perhaps life keeps pummeling you with cold, wet snowballs. Whatever it is, remember that your Creator is working all the details of your life together for good—even the bad stuff. When you rest in this truth, stressing about the unknown becomes unnecessary. God has it all mapped out, and His plans are always good.

So embrace the freedom that comes with trusting the Master Planner. He is with you every step of the way.

(And if you're curious whether Isaac won the challenge . . . well, watch the video!)

— JUSTIN

KNOWLEDGE IS POWER

O LORD, you have searched me and known me! You know when I sit down and when I rise up; you discern my thoughts from afar. You search out my path and my lying down and are acquainted with all my ways. Even before a word is on my tongue, behold, O LORD, you know it altogether.

—PSALM 139:1–4

When we make a JStu video, I know virtually everything about it before we start.

I know the concept, the flow, and all the production details like the date and filming location. Once the rough-cut video goes to editing, I know all the music, transitions, memes, and anything else we'll use in it. I know this video inside out before it's fully formed. How? Because I created the video from the start.

I also know the people on the JStu team pretty well because I'm with them almost every day. I know how they act. I know their likes and dislikes.

For instance, I know Isaac really enjoys music. He loves listening to new songs and finding new artists. I know that Justin, like me, enjoys stopping for coffee on long trips to distant filming locations. And I know he isn't the biggest sports fan, so I don't expect him to watch my beloved Denver Broncos with me on Sundays.

> GOD KNOWS HOW TO LOVINGLY GUIDE YOU WHERE YOU NEED TO GO AND TOWARD ADVENTURES YOU NEED TO TAKE.

Yep, I know a lot about JStu. But I'm also human, so I can't know everything. Sometimes things come up in video shoots that I didn't plan for. And sometimes Justin, Isaac, or another team member will do something that surprises me.

God, however, is never surprised! He knows everything about you because He created you. He knows how you think, what your interests are, and what you're capable of achieving. He knows you inside out.

This is great news because it means God knows everything you need. He knows how to help you through problems. He knows exactly where you excel and where you need to grow. He knows how to lovingly guide you where you need to go and toward adventures you need to take.

I'm confident God wants the best for me because He created me. He wants to see me thrive and do the best work I can do. You can have this confidence in Him too!

Life isn't always easy. We don't have complete knowledge about the future, other people, or even ourselves! But remember: God knows you in every way possible. In good times and bad, your Creator's always got your back!

— ANDREW

A PERFECT RECORD

The LORD of hosts is exalted in justice, and the Holy God shows himself holy in righteousness.
—ISAIAH 5:16

A little while back, we did a video where we built a homemade submarine. And I use the term *submarine* loosely! The plan was to transport the contraption across the country, plop it in the ocean, and survive inside it for a whole day at sea.

As you can imagine, this video presented many hurdles. For instance, none of us knew how to make a submarine—or even how to weld metal! Blake and Samuel from our build team had to take classes on welding to make the submarine. The end result wasn't a fully submersible vessel—just something that could be partially submerged underwater.

After months of building, we drove the submarine from Colorado to Florida and flew the whole JStu team down to film this epic adventure. The excitement level was high!

Unfortunately, as soon as the submarine hit the water, it began leaking. The welds weren't watertight, and the submarine was unusable. *Glub, glub, glub.*

Everyone was disappointed that our mission failed. However, we kept making repairs. After a few weeks, the submarine actually worked and we were able to film our video!

We all make mistakes and poor decisions in life. After all, we're human! Because of our failures, it can be hard to wrap our minds around a God who's never made a mistake *ever*. But these aspects of God's nature are super important for us to understand.

God is *holy*. This means He is above everything in His creation. He's on another level! And He is *perfect*—He cannot sin. God's righteousness means that He's always fair and always does what's right.

Like everyone else, you have areas where you struggle, things you fail at, and moments when you don't have the strength to overcome the challenges you face. That's okay! Those are the times when God reveals His power and goodness in truly amazing ways. Where we fail, God always succeeds. Where we are inadequate, He is perfectly capable. Where we are weak, He is strong (2 Corinthians 12:9–10).

So whenever your life feels like a sinking submarine, cry out to the God who is perfect, without sin, and always does what's right. He'll answer in ways you can't imagine.

—ANDREW

WHAT A SAVE!

> God has not destined us for wrath, but to obtain
> salvation through our Lord Jesus Christ.
> —1 THESSALONIANS 5:9

There's one JStu challenge that still sends shivers down my spine.

We built a massive volcano, and a crane dangled me in a locked metal cage thirty feet in the air over the bubbling abyss. My challenge was to escape the cage. Inside my metal prison were tools I could get to only by finding hidden keys.

Every fifteen minutes, the crane lowered me closer to the inside of the volcano, a giant hole filled with dry ice. (Real talk: if the carbon dioxide in dry ice is inhaled in large amounts, it can cause your heart to shut down.) Danger level? Off the charts.

Trying to escape the cage was crazy-hard! As the crane slowly lowered me into the depths, something inside me started to feel *off*. Breathing became a struggle, my heart raced, and panic set in. Trapped and running out of time, I was in real danger, and reality hit hard—I couldn't escape. That's when the team quickly pulled me to safety.

As I reflect on that experience, I see the parallels with God's rescue mission for us.

When we sin, that means we're making choices that aren't good for us. We put ourselves on a collision course with destruction (Romans 6:23). But God loves us so much, and He doesn't want that for us. So He's given us a path to safety, and He did it through the death and resurrection of His Son, Jesus Christ. It's a gift we neither earned nor deserve.

Just as my team pulled me from the simmering peril, God will lift us out of danger when we're trapped and helpless in our sin (all our choices that don't help us live with the wholeness and joy God wants for

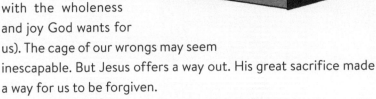

us). The cage of our wrongs may seem inescapable. But Jesus offers a way out. His great sacrifice made a way for us to be forgiven.

God dearly loves you, and He's a God who saves. So trust in the only One who can save you, and rest in the full protection of His love. His rescue is real. He's waiting for you.

— JUSTIN

CLOSER THAN YOU THINK

**The LORD is near to all who call on him,
to all who call on him in truth.**
—PSALM 145:18

Justin, Isaac, and I once did a video where we survived one hundred hours together in a bunker. Sounds pretty daunting, right? But to make it even more difficult, every twenty-four hours we entered a new bunker that was smaller than the previous one.

By the end of the video, we were crammed in a bunker that wasn't even big enough for us to stand up or lie down. Even with my eyes closed, I knew Justin and Isaac were near me. We were pretty much shoulder to shoulder. And we kept bumping into each other. The experience was definitely not for anyone with claustrophobia!

That whole experience was a little too close for comfort. On the other hand, I'm glad God is always near. And not just because He doesn't get smelly in close quarters!

Sometimes, though, it seems as if we're locked in a bunker and God is on the outside. Have you ever felt distant or disconnected from God? With everything going on in the world and in our heads and hearts, it can be hard to see and sense Him. But He's always there, ready for you to call out to Him so He can remove the walls closing in on you.

Even though He's invisible, God is always with us. He's present everywhere in His universe, and there's nowhere we can go where He doesn't exist (Psalm 139:7–12). The Old Testament prophet Elijah found that out firsthand when he had a vivid experience with God's nearness.

In 1 Kings 19, Elijah was running for his life from evil King Ahab and Queen Jezebel. As Elijah hid in a cave, an earthquake, a windstorm, and a fire appeared before him. But God was not in any of those powerful forces. Instead, God spoke to Elijah in a gentle whisper. He was close enough for His quiet voice to be heard.

God's nearness is personal—a one-on-one relationship. When we trust in Jesus, God actually sends His Spirit to live in us forever (1 Corinthians 3:16). That's super personal!

When God feels far away, call on Him. How? Pray to Him and search out the truths in His Word. He might answer you in a visible, undeniable way. But more often than not, He'll gently whisper to you through His loving Spirit in your heart.

— ANDREW

GOD'S NEARNESS IS PERSONAL.

27

IMAGE IS EVERYTHING

Then God said, "Let us make human beings in our image, to be like us."
—GENESIS 1:26 NLT

A few years ago, we decided to do a pop-up shop near a local high school and give away JStu Christmas sweaters. We pulled up next to the school at lunchtime to hand out as many sweaters as possible so the students could wear them in class.

We envisioned tons of kids walking the hallways all wearing JStu sweaters, while everyone without a sweater would ask where to get one and maybe even look us up online. The mission was a success! We handed out dozens of sweaters that day—and cleaned out some space at the office. Double-win!

All those kids wearing our sweaters were bearing the JStu image. They had become part of the JStu squad! Our fans like to rock our gear because they want to be part of our culture of fun and belong to our team.

That sense of JStu camaraderie, though, is nothing compared to the blessing of being an image-bearer of God! Did you know He makes every human being in His image, including you? Because God is a spirit, you don't physically look like Him, but you are still like Him in many ways.

As an image-bearer, you naturally share traits with God:

reason, speech, doing right instead of wrong, compassion, creativity—characteristics that nothing else in creation has. This gives you great worth and purpose, and it distinguishes you from the rocks and rivers, plants and planets, animals and algae.

As God's image-bearer, you represent Him. God wants you to show people who He is and what He is like.

What's more, being made in God's image means you get to have fellowship with God in a deeply personal way, filled with communication on both sides. What a privilege!

Image is everything. Because the Creator of the universe fashioned you in His likeness, you have tremendous value and purpose!

—ANDREW

TAKE A HIKE

Whether we're filming a video or just hanging out, we love getting outside and enjoying the giant playground God created. Time for you to do the same! Hiking is a great way to enjoy the wonders of our world, spend time with family and friends, and get some exercise.

GET PREPARED

1. Pick your hiking team. (Never go alone!)
2. Choose your hiking trail.
3. Check the weather and plan a day to hike.
4. Dress smart.
   - comfortable clothes that are suited to the day's weather forecast
   - comfortable walking shoes
   - hat
5. Pack a backpack with a survival kit.
   - first aid kit
   - water
   - food
   - trail map
   - smartphone
   - sunscreen
   - utility knife

6. Pack anything else you need for the weather or your chosen hike.

    raincoat
    field journal
    magnifying glass
    jacket
    warm hat, gloves, and scarf
    gloves for climbing or bouldering
    flashlight
    water shoes

Pro tip: Take photos with your smartphone or a camera to remember your adventure.

Next level:

- Find a trail that includes inclines, boulders, or water crossings.
- Find a trail that allows bikes, and ride instead of hike.
- Choose a short trail, and run the whole way.

THE ONE AND ONLY

This is eternal life, that they know you, the only true God, and Jesus Christ whom you have sent.
—JOHN 17:3

What if the delivery driver at your door isn't *actually* a delivery driver?

That's exactly what happened to several of our local fans who bought merch from our online store. For a unique video, we transformed ourselves into delivery drivers and personally delivered orders. When we showed up at their doors, they were confused, shocked, and excited all at once! For us, it was a fun way to surprise and personally thank some fans who support us.

Playing pretend is something we've all done from our earliest years. (And some of us continue to do it as adults!) Whether it's going to an imaginary restaurant with plastic food or dressing up as a favorite superhero, we've all faked it for fun!

But here's a big truth package delivered right to your doorstep: the God of the Bible is no pretender. In fact, He's the one true God.

There are thousands (yes, thousands!) of religions in the world. Yet there is no one like our God. He is the *only* true God.

I know what you might be thinking: *Yeah, okay, but how do we really know for sure?* You don't have to take our word for it. Lots of brilliant people who study science, history, philosophy, and other smart things can point you to a million reasons they believe this—everything from the perfect design of insect wings to ancient artifacts. Some even point to love as their reason to believe in God.

The Bible is pretty clear too. Even though it was written by a bunch of different people over thousands of years, its message is clear and consistent: God is real. He's in charge. And He loves you a ton.

Want to hear something even more amazing? The one true God of the universe wants to have a relationship with His creation. He gave us the Bible so we can hear His words as He speaks directly to us. He guides us with wisdom as we turn the pages, and He promises to light our paths as we take steps in the unknown.

Real talk: if someone knocks on my door when I'm not expecting guests, I'm reluctant to answer. But when God knocks on the door of your heart with His truth, open the door! As Jesus says, "I stand at the door and knock. If anyone hears my voice and opens the door, I will come in to him and eat with him, and he with me" (Revelation 3:20).

Knock, knock . . .

God—the only true God—is at your door, calling you to trust in Him. Don't shut Him out. Let Him in!

—JUSTIN

ONE TRUE FAITH

Jesus said to him, "I am the way, and the truth, and the life. No one comes to the Father except through me."
—JOHN 14:6

Have you ever been at a restaurant thinking you ordered one thing, but the server handed you something else instead?

Once on a trip to New York with my wife, I wanted a tasty burger. Following my craving, we accidentally stumbled into a vegan restaurant. No beef, chicken, pork, or any other animal-based products. Everything, including the "meat," was made from plants. There's nothing wrong with that; it just caught me by surprise. Confused but curious, I sat down, wondering if the burgers would taste anything like what I'm used to.

I took one bite . . . and to my surprise, it tasted like a real meat burger! It looked, felt, and even smelled like the genuine thing.

Still, no matter how close a vegan burger comes to imitating a burger made of meat, it's still not the real deal. There's just something about a big, juicy, delicious beef burger. *Mmmm . . .*

Wait, where was I? Ah, yes . . . imitations. So how are vegan burgers like religions? There are countless belief systems out there and lots of imitations, but Christianity is the one true faith. It's the only faith that delivers what it promises—eternal life with God for those who follow Jesus.

Lots of religions look pretty similar. And throughout your life you'll probably run across people who believe religions are all the same. You might even hear the common phrase that "many roads lead to heaven."

But it's just not true.

Like comparing a real burger to a vegan version, it's important to go beyond the surface of religion. You need to examine the ingredients, so to speak—the source of its alleged truth, where it came from, and what it's made of. You need to be able to spot counterfeits. Otherwise you run the risk of swallowing a fake while believing it's the real deal.

At their core, all other world religions focus on humans trying to reach up to heaven on their own—through good works, enlightenment, sacrifice, etc. But Christianity is the only faith that says heaven reaches down to us. Only in Christianity will you find the true message that we *can't* do it on our own. We need God's help to reach heaven and to live the way He wants us to here on earth.

Jesus spelled it out clearly in John 14:6. He is the only way to God—no ifs, ands, or buts. Salvation is possible only through faith in Jesus, who died for our sins and rose again to give us new life.

Don't settle for imitations (though I have to say, vegan burgers can be delicious!). Find the truth about life, salvation, and eternity in God's perfect Word. Find life in Jesus. He's the real deal.

— JUSTIN

ABSOLUTE TRUTH? ABSOLUTELY!

> "Make them holy by your truth; teach
> them your word, which is truth."
> —JOHN 17:17 NLT

Do you like spending time at the library? I sure do, though my visits tend to be a bit unconventional.

We've staged several JStu videos at the library. From playing hide-and-seek to eating loudly next to people trying to study to even shaving Andrew's head—let's just say we might not be model library-goers.

Even though our JStu library adventures are all about laughs and fun, I always come away amazed at the sheer expanse of books lining the shelves. Going to the library is like entering a massive maze of literature, with answers to questions about a zillion different things.

It makes me wonder: How many people go to the library searching for answers about eternity?

After all, you can find books on virtually every topic in the library, including religion and spiritual matters. The shelves are full of bestsellers and books whose authors claim to be experts in psychology and spirituality. But of course, many of those "experts" disagree. What we really need is one big book with all the true answers in one place. Right?

Well, here's the good news: this book exists—it's the Bible! It's a *giant* book, and God put all the things He wants us to know inside. God gifted us His Word so that we would know right from wrong, truth from fake stuff, and certainty instead of doubt. He gave us the Bible because He loves us and wants us to know Him.

God tells us to think about His Word day and night, and that's not a random suggestion. He knows it's easy to fall for lies, so He wants us to know the truth. When lies, false beliefs, and selfish hopes fill our minds with clatter and distraction, His truth is a clear-sounding bell we can tune in to as we try to figure out where to go. As we journey through life, God's Word helps us walk with confidence as we remember the One who created us and His Son, Jesus, who died to save us.

The world is full of competing ideas. Everywhere you turn, people are telling you how to act, what to do, and what to believe. There's no end to the different opinions, values, and beliefs that are vying for your attention and commitment.

When you don't know where to turn with your questions, remember there's one book that has the answers—the Bible. If video games are more your thing, think of God's Word more like a divinely inspired cheat code, helping you break through the noise and win at the game of life. And that's the absolute truth.

— JUSTIN

LET'S GET PERSONAL

See what kind of love the Father has given to us, that we should be called children of God; and so we are.

—1 JOHN 3:1

How did you first hear about God? Maybe it was through a friend at school or a neighbor or your parents. Or maybe you're just now hearing about God through this book! (So cool!)

I don't remember a time when I wasn't hearing about God. I grew up with parents who were Christians. I was baptized as a baby and went to church every Sunday when I was a kid. In high school, I joined some Christian groups and went to Bible studies. I definitely wasn't a perfect kid, but I tried to do the right things.

Then I went to college. I had lived in the same house my whole life, so moving away to college was a big deal. And I wasn't totally comfortable being on my own. I found myself needing someone to lean on. I needed someone who would always be there for me no matter where I was physically. I also began to truly understand the reality that I am a sinner in need of a Savior. I found all of this in God and His Son, Jesus Christ. I became more than a "good person" who went to church. I found a personal relationship with Jesus.

One of the greatest truths of Scripture is that God wants a personal relationship with us. Salvation isn't just an impersonal transaction, like earning a high grade on a test or putting money in the bank. When you trust in Jesus to forgive your sins, you don't get a trophy or a certificate of achievement. You get something far greater: you become a child of God.

This gift speaks to the love and tenderness of God. He's never far away from us. He's always near and personal. Yes, He may be the Ruler of heaven and earth. But God is also a caring, compassionate Father. And for the children He adopts into His heavenly family, His love is beyond description. What a blessing to have that kind of love from such a big God!

After placing my faith in Jesus, I got baptized again because I understood more clearly what it means to follow Christ. I'm still growing in my faith each week and trying to become more like Him.

Maybe you grew up in church like I did. Or maybe your story is different from mine. Either way, God wants to have a personal relationship with you too! If you haven't entered God's family yet through faith in Jesus, you can do so today! And if you already have, that's awesome!

No matter what your story is, remember that God loves you dearly. He's not a distant deity. He's a close, personal heavenly Father. Through Jesus, you can be a beloved child of the King of the universe. How cool is *that*?

—ANDREW

A SORRY SITUATION

> For God so loved the world, that he gave his only Son, that whoever believes in him should not perish but have eternal life.
>
> —JOHN 3:16

Few things make better comedy than awkward moments. Like when you trip and fall in the school hallway and the contents of your backpack spill all over the floor. Or when the ticket booth employee says, "Enjoy your movie," and you reply, "Thanks, you too!"

I've had my fair share of awkward moments. In fact, we took awkwardness to the extreme and made a hilarious video about apologizing to strangers for no reason whatsoever. Whether it was in the supermarket, in the library, or outside buildings on a college campus, we approached complete strangers and said, "I'm so sorry." The reactions were priceless—everything from "Why?" to confused looks to "Who *are* you?"

Apologizing for nothing is hilarious. But it feels a little different when you *do* have something to be sorry for, doesn't it?

We've talked about sin a little bit—that's when we make choices that don't line up with what God wants for us. Unfortunately, we humans are *really* good at sinning. Which means there's always something we need to be forgiven for.

Since Adam and Eve disobeyed God, sin has created a gap between us and our Creator. What's worse, sometimes we deceive ourselves into thinking what we've done isn't that bad, that we don't need God's forgiveness. We might think, *I'm generally a good person. It's not like I've seriously hurt anyone.* Yet God's Word reminds us that everyone does bad things and no one meets God's standard of perfection (Romans 3:23).

But amid all this bad news, we're met with the *best* truth of all time: God wants to save us anyway. And He has given us a way to be saved! How'd He do that? By sending His Son, Jesus Christ, to live a perfect life for us and pay for our sins. God is a saving God—and He always has been.

Even as believers, we'll still fall short daily. But here's more good news: in those moments, we can ask for God's forgiveness and He will give it. Because Jesus paid fully for *all* our sins. Wow!

So the next time you find yourself apologizing for something you've done, remember the incredible message of the gospel. Say you're sorry for your sins to God, have faith in Jesus, and experience God's forgiveness.

— JUSTIN

FAITH THAT FLOATS

**For by grace you have been saved through faith.
And this is not your own doing; it is the gift of God,
not a result of works, so that no one may boast.**
—EPHESIANS 2:8–9

One of our most memorable adventures was our attempt to build a working "submarine" from scratch. Andrew shared about it some in Day 7, but maybe you didn't catch just how crazy this project was!

It all started as an idea to set sail—and survive!—on a local lake in Colorado. But on launch day, I couldn't make it, and the submarine sprung a major leak.

Our team was discouraged, but not defeated. Our brilliant build team went back to work, tirelessly constructing, testing, and modifying the vessel until it was ready. Once JStu Submarine 2.0 was finished, our video editor Rick drove the updated contraption twenty-two hours cross-country to Florida. Andrew and I planned to survive for thirty hours submerged in the Gulf of Mexico!

After more leaks, setbacks, and delays—and a considerable dent in our wallets—we finally set sail and accomplished our mission! But it took a ton of time and effort from a remarkable group of people. We never could've done it by ourselves.

The same is true with our salvation. We are born with a

rebellious nature, thinking we don't need anybody else—including God. It's just part of being human. We start life sinking under the weight of our sins, and we simply can't save ourselves.

Enter Jesus.

God's Son is the key to the whole voyage of life. Because it's not about what we can do; it's about what Jesus has *already* done. On the cross, Jesus gave His life. He paid the price we could never pay and took all of God's righteous punishment for our sins. Then Jesus rose from the dead, offering us new life through *His* new life.

Are you sinking under the weight of your own attempts to stay afloat in life? Cut the anchor of trying so hard, and set sail with Jesus! He transforms our leaky hearts into spiritually ship-shape vessels that can weather life's storms, all for His glory and our good. With Jesus as your captain, you can't go wrong.

— JUSTIN

GIZMOS AND GLORY

Bring all who claim me as their God, for I have made them for my glory. It was I who created them.

—ISAIAH 43:7 NLT

Have you ever had an idea that seemed amazing in your head, only to watch it fail miserably in real life?

Yeah, me too.

Take our Bike Build Battle. Andrew, Isaac, and I were on a mission to craft our dream bikes from scratch. Thanks to a favorable ball drop on our Plinko board, we each got $1,000 to work with! In other words, if our bikes failed to roll, collapsed underneath us, or caused sudden death . . . well, we couldn't blame the budget.

I went all-in, using wood, mini utility tires, and plastic pipes—basically, the how-to guide for building real bikes—to construct a marvel of modern engineering.

Or so I thought.

Spoiler alert: it was a hilarious disaster. My bike barely budged and it ended up snapping into pieces underneath me. (But I ended up beating one of the other guys. Watch the video to find out who!) I tried to create a two-wheel wonder, but it ended up being a big *doh!* destined for the dumpster.

Now let's shift gears a bit. (See what I did there?) Let's talk about a far better creation: you and me! God, the Grand Designer,

created you as a true marvel of originality, care, and love. And He also gave you great purpose. As Isaiah 43:7 says, He created you for His glory.

How mind-blowing is that? God, in all His power and magnificence, intentionally handcrafted each one of us to show off His awesome goodness.

Being made for God's glory means that your very existence brings God great praise. That in and of itself is super cool. But there's even more to it! Not only do you bring God glory simply by *being*, but you can also pile up His praises by what you *do*. Your goal—your whole purpose on earth—is to worship God, glorify Him, and enjoy the ride forever. Now that's some serious purpose!

No one will ever ask me to build a bike for them. But unlike my comedy of errors, you are not a mistake. Quite the opposite! When God made you, He knew exactly what He was doing. He knew your life could shine a light on His indescribable wisdom, power, and love. Wow. Isn't that the kind of Creator you want to represent?

Homemade bike builds may fail . . . but you don't have to! As you roll through life, remember your high calling: to worship and glorify your Creator forever. And to have fun—and laugh—daily!

— JUSTIN

WRITTEN IN HIS BOOK

I saw the dead, great and small, standing before the throne, and books were opened. Then another book was opened, which is the book of life. And the dead were judged by what was written in the books, according to what they had done.

—REVELATION 20:12

In our early years on YouTube, we were known for our goofy public pranks. We've done it all—surprising people with puppets, spilling a fake cake on unsuspecting victims, startling folks with a whoopee cushion, and much more. Many of our tricks have been hilariously successful. But some definitely did not go according to plan. I've looked back and asked myself, *What was I thinking?*

In one video, we walked past people as we ripped out big, meaty burps. Sounds funny and lighthearted, right? Well, not everyone thought so. One guy was *really* mad at Andrew. Oops. Maybe that wasn't the best idea.

Our choices matter. They affect you and those around you. Your choices can hurt or help. They can even change your future.

At the end of our lives, God will judge each of us according to the choices we make, both good and bad. So who decides what's good and bad? God does! As the Creator of all things, He makes the rules. And He tells us what they are—what pleases Him and what doesn't—in Scripture.

But remember: our salvation isn't based on good works. There's nothing we can do to earn God's favor or pay for our sins. That only comes through Jesus' death and resurrection. Praise God for this free gift of salvation! The most important choice you can ever make is to trust in Jesus for forgiveness.

You can choose to believe that the Bible is true, that what God wants for you is good, and that you need forgiveness. Or you can choose not to believe that.

The negative reactions to some of our YouTube pranks caused us to make a choice, and we began focusing on other ways to laugh daily. What choices are you making in life? Choose to make the best decision ever: trust in God's Word.

— JUSTIN

THE MOST IMPORTANT CHOICE YOU CAN EVER MAKE IS TO TRUST IN JESUS FOR FORGIVENESS.

WHAT GOD REALLY CARES ABOUT

Yet you have made him a little lower than the heavenly beings and crowned him with glory and honor.

—PSALM 8:5

Years ago, we had a goal of reaching one million YouTube subscribers. Our fans got in on the fun and created a challenge called "Bald Andy." If we hit the one million mark, I had to completely shave my head. To up the ante and make it more cringe, we decided that my hair-removal experience would happen in a busy public library.

I had been growing out my hair in nervous anticipation of the milestone, and when the big day came, I took my luscious locks to the library. After sitting next to some complete strangers, I whipped out an electric razor and started shearing myself like a sheep. The onlookers were stunned, and it was really embarrassing. Worse yet, we didn't even complete the video that day!

I spent the rest of the evening and next morning with rando bald spots all over my head. I looked hideous, like some sort of freaky Halloween character. Even after the full shave, my wife was not a fan. (Sorry, honey.) Fortunately, my hair grows quickly, and my debonair do was back in action a few months later.

Being bald wasn't my best look. But thankfully, God doesn't measure our worth by looks or any other external standards (1 Samuel 16:7). Neither does He measure it by our intelligence, athletic abilities, musical skills, popularity, or social media followers. Our value is directly and permanently linked to being made in His image. Because of that, you are invaluable!

Our true worth can be hard to understand since our values are often tied to what we can see, touch, taste, hear, and physically experience. But God defines values differently. You are worthy of His love no matter what you do or what you look like. You are worthy because of who you are—His child.

Consider this: God created an entire world for you to explore and enjoy. He's done wonders for you that even angels are curious about (1 Peter 1:12). His love for you is greater than the expanse between earth and the farthest reaches of outer space (Psalm 103:11). And He wants to spend eternity with you, so He gave up what was most precious to Him—His own Son—to make it possible.

For you, He spared no expense!

Don't let other people define your image. Rest in the immeasurable value and worth God has given you. You bear His image. And that's enough.

—ANDREW

THE ETERNALS

"An hour is coming when all who are in the tombs will hear his voice and come out, those who have done good to the resurrection of life, and those who have done evil to the resurrection of judgment."

—JOHN 5:28–29

There have been two times while making JStu videos that I actually thought, *This might be the end*.

The first was when we took our homemade submarine out to sea. The night before, all I could think about was the contraption flipping over and sinking with Justin and me stuck inside. I was beyond nervous. Thankfully we survived . . . and got a great video!

The other time was during our overnight stay in "the world's most dangerous hotel." It's a creaky, old lighthouse in the middle of the Atlantic Ocean, thirty-five miles from shore. You won't see this little nugget in the video, but moments before I swung out above the water on a homemade rope swing, the lighthouse owner found a malfunction in the cord. He quickly replaced it and said it was good to go, but I was rattled. If the cord had snapped with me on the swing, I would've fallen several stories into shark-infested waters. Yikes!

Moments like these are vivid reminders of how fragile and

transient this life is. Praise God that there's more to our existence than our time here on earth!

Jesus' words in John 5:28–29 remind us that there is life after death. We are eternal beings. Our physical bodies will fade away, but our souls will live forever. This is good news!

But Jesus' words also contain a warning of judgment. One day every human being, including you, will stand before God's throne. And there are really only two ways to go. Those who have trusted in Jesus for the forgiveness of their sins will receive "the resurrection of life." But those who have rejected Him will receive "the resurrection of judgment." The best option is pretty clear!

Death isn't fun to think about, whether you're filming videos at sea or just chilling at home. But Jesus removes our fear of death! When we trust in Him, we can rest assured that God will raise us to life in His presence forever!

I don't know how or when I'm going to peace out of this life. I hope I have some good time left to make epic videos. But I know that when I do go, eternity with God awaits. That fills me with peace—and if you trust Jesus, this peace can be yours too!

— ANDREW

SKATEBOARD BUILD

God is a maker! And as His creation, we have a similar desire to design, craft, and build (even though we need supplies to start with, unlike God!). Whether it's underground bunkers, treehouses, submarines, or even coffins, we at JStu are all about building stuff.

Your challenge is to build your own skateboard from scratch!

TOOLS

jigsaw, band saw, or handsaw

vise grip

electric sander or sanding block

carpenter's square

power drill

drill bit (same diameter as wheel truck bolts)

countersink drill bit (same diameter as wheel truck bolts)

Phillips screwdriver

adjustable wrench

utility knife

SUPPLIES

one 2' x 8' board, cut to 30 inches

a set of two 7.13mm skate trucks with wheels and hardware (tip: purchase a preassembled set online or at a local skate shop)

pencil

high-grit sandpaper

low-grit sandpaper

masking tape

one 30-inch strip of skateboard grip tape

INSTRUCTIONS

1. Draw rounded corners on the board to make the shape you'd like your skateboard to be.
2. Use a saw to cut along the pencil lines.
3. Place your board deck into a vise grip and tighten. Sand all surfaces and edges of the board with the high-grit paper, followed by the low-grit paper, until smooth.
4. Lay the board on a flat surface with the underside up. Measure six inches from one tip of the board and make a pencil mark. Align a carpenter's square to your mark

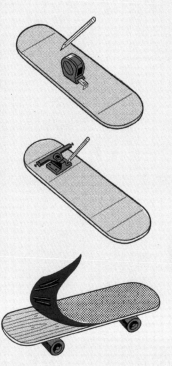

and one side of the board. Draw a line across the board from one side to the other. Repeat for the other end.

5. Place a wheel truck with its long side straight along one line. In each hole in the truck frame, make a pencil mark. Repeat on the other end.

6. On each pencil mark, drill a hole straight through the deck. There will be eight holes total.

7. Replace your regular drill bit with the countersink drill bit. Flip the deck over to the top side, and drill into each hole until the flat top of the bit is flush with the wood.

8. Insert all eight bolts through their holes from the top of the deck. If the bolt heads stick up from the wood, drill deeper with the countersink bit.

9. Cover the bolt heads with masking tape. Flip the board over so the underside faces up.

10. Place the wheel trucks by guiding the truck's holes over the bolts.

11. Tighten the nuts onto each bolt with the wrench. Remove the tape.

12. Place your board top-down on the grip tape. Trace around your board and use a utility knife to cut out the tape. Affix the grip tape to the top surface of your deck.

Pro tip: Before using any power tools, learn how to use them safely and ask an adult for help.

Next level: Design your own artwork on the underside. Draw, paint, apply decals—whatever you think will look awesome!

BEFORE THE DONUT HOUSE

> And he is before all things, and in him all things hold together.
> —COLOSSIANS 1:17

When you watch our videos, we want you to laugh and enjoy the goofiness and crazy adventures you see onscreen. We don't often show the work that goes into creating our content. But for some videos, we work *hundreds* of hours to put it all together. We work hard to make you smile!

To create our donut house, our build team spent months planning and crafting. Day after day, they constructed a massive four-room living space in the shape of a donut—a never-before-seen masterpiece. While the team tirelessly worked on this ultimate nonedible treat, we filmed other projects.

The end result was spectacular (minus a few leaks and no heat!). As we walked through the donut house, we truly felt as if we were living inside the world's biggest Krispy Kreme. There was even a hole in the middle for our "backyard"! With four beds, a bathroom, and a gaming room, the donut house was one of our coolest JStu creations ever. When I showed the finished project to some friends, they were amazed. But they had no idea about all the effort that made it possible.

Sometimes I treat Jesus' life kind of like my friends saw the donut house. I focus only on the obvious: His birth, life, death, and resurrection. And make no mistake, these are *HUGE*! His work on earth provides our salvation.

But have you ever thought about how Jesus "got there"? Because if you look in Scripture, you'll find that there's a lot more to Jesus behind the scenes.

Jesus didn't just appear as a miracle baby in Bethlehem. As the eternal Son of God, He already existed. Jesus is part of what's called the Holy Trinity, which is a way of describing the three "persons" that are part of who God is. There's God the Father, God the Son (Jesus), and God the Holy Spirit. So Jesus never had a beginning. He's not a created being like we are. And He'll never have an end. He has just always *been*. Chew on that for a while.

In fact, it was actually Jesus who created the world and continues to create all the beauty around us (Colossians 1:15–17). Everything exists in Him, and He holds the universe together.

Jesus, the eternal Son of God, is holding your life together too. Sometimes it will seem like things in your life are falling apart. But if you follow Jesus, He will always be working behind the scenes to hold you together. You're in the hands of the best craftsman in the universe! So trust Jesus and enjoy the masterpiece He's creating in your life. His work will never leak!

— JUSTIN

CHECK OUT WHAT THE BIBLE HAS TO SAY ABOUT JESUS' ETERNAL NATURE.
- JOHN 1:1–3
- COLOSSIANS 1:15–20
- HEBREWS 1:2
- REVELATION 22:13

THE DEAL OF A LIFETIME

He died in our place to take away our sins, and not only our sins but the sins of all people.
—1 JOHN 2:2 NCV

Throughout the years, Andrew and I have amassed quite a collection of trading cards. Our YouTube channel has several unboxing videos where we splurged on pricey trading card packs, hoping to strike gold. More often than not, we hit the jackpot!

Once, we even discovered a signed and numbered card of NBA All-Star Kobe Bryant. It's a one-of-a-kind collectible that could be worth an insane $25,000 or more if sold to the right collector. We were beyond thrilled! Picture two grown men gleefully sprinting around a warehouse as if they'd won the lottery.

But here's the kicker: the card is only as valuable as what someone's willing to exchange for it. If no one wants it, then it's just a fancy piece of cardboard sitting in a closet. But if a collector wants to trade something to purchase it (such as $25,000!), then it becomes extremely valuable.

But even a high-dollar card-for-cash trade like that pales in comparison to the most extraordinary exchange in history—Jesus trading His perfect life for ours so that we can live with God forever. That's how much you're worth to Jesus!

When you trade collectibles, you expect to come out of the

> JESUS TOOK THE BAD, AND WE GET THE GOOD. IT'S THE DEAL OF A LIFETIME!

trade with something of equal value. But when Jesus died on the cross, He took all our wrongs upon Himself so that we could stand as if we were perfect before God. Jesus took the bad, and we get the good. It's the deal of a lifetime!

Through this exchange of the ages, Jesus purchased salvation for us along with adoption as God's children, eternal life with Him, and so much more! To receive this free trade—this amazing gift of salvation—all we have to do is turn away from living for ourselves and turn to follow Jesus.

Andrew and I cherish that rare Kobe Bryant card. Maybe we'll trade it one day. Maybe not. But we'll always have the most valuable possession in the galaxy—the ultimate All-Star Savior.

Whatever you do, take the trade Jesus is offering you! It's real, it's free, and it's waiting for you.

— JUSTIN

REAL ONES

> **"For even the Son of Man came not to be served but to serve, and to give his life as a ransom for many."**
> —MARK 10:45

Andrew and I started our channel small, with just the two of us juggling construction, filming, and editing. But truth be told, our building skills were shaky, and our editing was, well, a bit basic. As our YouTube views skyrocketed, we seized the opportunity to expand our team and brought in experts to cover our weak spots. From a rock-star editing team to a talented construction crew and a top-notch production squad, these unsung heroes work tirelessly off screen to help our videos hit new heights.

Andrew and I get the majority of screen time, but the real MVPs are the people you don't see. They build crazy, out-of-this-world sets, clean up our messes, and spend extra hours making the high-quality edits behind the scenes each week. They don't look for glory; they just want to see JStu succeed.

This mindset mirrors how humble Jesus is. He's the best example we have for what it looks like to be a humble servant. He left heaven's glory to come to this dirty, messy, painful world. He had every right to come as a king and be served, but He chose a life of poverty, service, and suffering.

While He was on earth, Jesus intentionally looked for ways

to meet needs, whether it was a visible miracle or an inner transformation. He healed diseases, washed His disciples' dusty feet, and gave up His own life to purchase our freedom from sin and death. Wow. It's amazing to think we serve a God who loves us that much.

When we serve without looking for reward, we show others what Jesus' humble servant heart looks like. Jesus said it's better to give than to receive (Acts 20:35), and shifting our focus from ourselves to others transforms our hearts.

Today, I challenge you to live out this truth. Don't seek your own glory. Instead, find creative ways to serve others—a neighbor, family member, friend, or even a stranger. Opportunities are everywhere, and your helping impact is immeasurable. Serving not only blesses others; it also brings you joy and fulfillment. So embrace the beauty of serving, and watch how God works through you and in you!

— JUSTIN

SHIFTING OUR FOCUS FROM OURSELVES
TO OTHERS TRANSFORMS OUR HEARTS.

YOUR LIGHTHOUSE

Without faith it is impossible to please him, for whoever would draw near to God must believe that he exists and that he rewards those who seek him.
—HEBREWS 11:6

In 2023, Justin, Isaac, and I took one of the craziest trips of our JStu career. We went to Iceland! Our mission was to spend twenty-four hours in a lighthouse.

Now, I know what you're thinking: *Uh . . . there are tons of lighthouses in America.* That's true. (You genius, you.) But we wanted to visit the Thridrangar Lighthouse, the most dangerous lighthouse in the world!

Thridrangar sits atop a skinny rock formation that juts more than one hundred feet above the icy waters of the northern Atlantic Ocean. It's more than four miles off Iceland's coast! The only way to get there is by helicopter, and because of the extreme dangers involved—including a helipad roughly the size of a bloated starfish—only one pilot in Iceland will fly there.

Breathe in, breathe out, breathe in, breathe out . . .

As we were preparing to fly out, we were all pretty nervous. It took a lot of faith to get into that helicopter, especially since we had only met the pilot a couple minutes before takeoff! We had to have faith in his flying skills. We had to have faith in God's protection. We had to have faith that the weather wouldn't be a threat.

And once at Thridrangar, we had to have faith that we wouldn't be attacked by the countless and very bad-tempered barfing birds. But that's a whole other story.

Faith was essential for our trip to Thridrangar Lighthouse. It's also a critical trait of being a Christian. The Bible defines faith as "confidence in what we hope for and assurance about what we do not see" (Hebrews 11:1). In other words, faith is believing in something that's not immediately evident with your eyes or experience. Christians need to have faith that God exists and that He is who He says He is, even though we can't see Him.

You can't see God in your bedroom or at the kitchen table or at school. Likewise, many of His promises are still unseen—they haven't happened yet. All of this requires faith!

Faith isn't always easy. But to grow closer to God, you have to have faith that He's real and that all His promises in the Bible are true.

Any trip to a dangerous place like the Thridrangar Lighthouse takes some solid faith. But faith in the unseen God of the universe? Now that's truly epic!

—ANDREW

FAITH: IT WORKS!

Faith by itself, if it does not have works, is dead.
—JAMES 2:17

What's your biggest fear? Sharks? Spiders? The dark? Speaking in public? Being served broccoli casserole for dinner? Me and a few of the JStu guys discovered that sleeping on the side of a cliff was scarier than anything we'd done before.

This was no wimpy pile of dirt. This was a huge precipice, hundreds of feet high, where we perched on a platform attached to the sheer rock face.

To pull off this insane video, we climbed a giant mountain in Estes Park, Colorado. Then we rappelled down the vertical cliff face until we reached a platform jutting out perpendicular to the mountainside, bolted into the rock. *That's* where our bed was. Oh, and the platform was kind of bouncy! I still get shivers just thinking about it.

It was hard making that initial decision to go over the cliff edge and rappel down the side! I had to take literal steps of faith, trusting my harness and rope, trusting the platform below, and trusting my companions. I didn't actually know what would happen, but I hoped for the best.

Climbing down a cliff is similar to our walk with God. James 2 describes the important relationship between our faith and our

actions. Salvation from sin comes only through trusting in Jesus as our Lord and Savior (John 20:31). That's faith. Then out of that faith, we do good works that reveal our changed heart, our love for God, and our obedience to Him. Good deeds don't save us, but they do reveal genuine faith.

The JStu guys and I could've talked all day long about making that crazy sleeping-on-the-side-of-a-cliff video. But until we did it—until we actually took those steps over the edge—our words were weak. Faith produced actions, and those actions demonstrated our faith.

Similarly, your faith in Jesus should produce God-glorifying action. Does your life show that you've been changed by Jesus, or are you just talking the talk? Genuine faith results in good works that honor God and point others to Him. Your good works don't earn you brownie points with God. But they will be a powerful testimony to others and will strengthen your own Christian walk.

With God's help, you can take big steps of faith and conquer the imposing mountains of life. Then, like us JStu guys on the side of that cliff, you can admire the view and praise God for the good work He's doing in your life.

—JUSTIN

GLORIOUS PURPOSE

So, whether you eat or drink, or whatever you do, do all to the glory of God.
—1 CORINTHIANS 10:31

What's your purpose in life? Are you here to get the most followers on TikTok or YouTube? To win every game you play? To make the most money possible?

You might decide one of these goals or another is your mission in life. But your true purpose is the one God gave you when He created you: you are here to glorify Him!

To glorify God means to praise and worship Him. It means bringing attention to Him, not yourself. It means to reflect His greatness in what you think, say, and do.

Everyone goes about this job in different ways. At JStu, we use our YouTube channel to glorify God. Sure, it's our job. But ultimately, it's about something more.

In an online world that can feel like a bottomless pit of negativity, we have made it our mission to be different. We want our channel to be a light in the darkness, a place filled with content that brings people joy, laughter, and lots of smiles.

It seems like everything online these days is about *me, me, me*—a world of self-promotion. We want our videos instead to point to *God, God, God!* We don't specifically talk about spiritual matters in most of our videos, but we do want our words and actions to glorify God. Proverbs 17:22 says, "A joyful heart is good medicine, but a crushed spirit dries up the bones." This verse guides our content, and it also inspired our motto of Laugh Daily. While we won't ever know the full impact our videos have, we have received messages saying they have drawn people closer to God. A few people have even been inspired to get baptized. Now that's cool!

What about you? How can you glorify God? You don't have to be a missionary, a pastor, or a YouTuber to honor Him. Just do the things God made you passionate about. And good news: you can do those things right where you are.

Notice what 1 Corinthians 10:31 says: "Do *all* to the glory of God." This includes everything in life, even down to the simple daily activities of eating and drinking. Everything you do should bring God praise, even the small stuff!

So whether it's drawing a picture, doing a chore, inviting a friend to church, or helping a neighbor with yard work, do it for the Lord! From the big stuff to the small, your life can show others His glory.

— ANDREW

RESET

"If you love me, you will keep my commandments."
—JOHN 14:15

When I was a kid, I loved eating pepperoni. But back in the day, we didn't have easy-to-open packages like we do now. You had to cut open the bag with a knife or scissors. I was supposed to ask my mom for help, but one day I was starving! I tried to open the package with a knife. Next stop: the hospital. I had to get stitches in my finger.

Fast-forward twenty-five years. My wife told my son many times to stop playing with a glass spray bottle. But he didn't listen. He fell and the bottle broke in his hand. Want to guess where the next stop was? Yep! The hospital for stitches. And you'd better believe he heard my pepperoni story!

Your parents have rules because they love you. They want to protect you, and they often know what's best for you. They know what happens when kids try to open the pepperoni package with a knife or play with a glass bottle.

The same is true with God. He has provided rules in the Bible because He loves you, wants to protect you, and knows what's best for you. He knows what will happen if you disobey.

Obedience is something all of us have to learn—often the hard way! It doesn't come naturally to us. Ever since Adam and Eve disobeyed God in the garden of Eden, every human's default setting, sadly, is to rebel against God.

Jesus came to save us from that deadly path. He came to reset our hearts and give us a new default setting—a heart that wants to obey and follow God.

Jesus said, "If you love me, you will keep my commandments." When you understand how much Jesus loves you and what He did to save you, it becomes much easier to do what He says.

We don't obey God to earn our salvation or His favor. Jesus has already done that for us through His death and resurrection. Instead, we obey God out of grateful hearts! If you love Jesus, you'll obey His commandments because you want to honor and praise Him.

Don't try to open pepperoni packages with a knife, don't play with glass bottles, and don't rebel against God! If you love Jesus and want to follow Him, trust Him and obey His commands. He always has your best in mind.

— ANDREW

JESUS CAME TO RESET OUR HEARTS.

GO BANANAS

But the fruit of the Spirit is love, joy, peace, patience, kindness, goodness, faithfulness, gentleness, self-control; against such things there is no law.
—GALATIANS 5:22–23

What's your favorite fruit? Apples, oranges, strawberries, kiwis, pineapples, or perhaps something else? We love bananas!

One day, we dressed up as life-size bananas, drove to the local grocery store, and bought all the bananas in the store (two overflowing shopping carts' worth!). We didn't want to leave any of our potassium-packed brothers behind! Then we handed out the bananas all over town. I guess you could say we went *bananas* with our bananas (*oof*). We do this stuff because we love our fans . . . a bunch (double-*oof*).

All jokes aside, this discussion is ripe with spiritual truth. (Sorry, couldn't help myself.) While physical fruit is really good for you—and a great source of video entertainment—spiritual fruit is truly where it's at!

As a follower of Jesus, you should be trying to develop all the fruits of the Spirit in your life, as described in Galatians 5:22–23. These "fruits" are godly character traits that every Christian should have: love, joy, peace, patience, kindness, goodness, faithfulness, gentleness, and self-control. Just like people recognized us in that video as, uh, bananas because of our fruity yellow bodysuits, people should recognize you as a follower of Jesus by seeing these spiritual qualities in your life.

In agriculture, the quality of the fruit shows if a plant or tree is healthy. You can know that a plant with fruit has strong roots, good nutrients, and the right amount of sun and water. Good tree = good fruit. Bad tree = bad fruit. When you're planted in Jesus and nourishing yourself with prayer, His Word, and strong Christian fellowship, good spiritual fruit will start to appear. This fruit will be evidence of a growing relationship with the Lord.

Just like apple trees don't produce apples overnight, spiritual fruit doesn't magically appear in an instant. It takes time. The more you pursue Jesus, the more you'll see love, joy, peace, patience, and all the other spiritual fruits blossom in your life.

Are you excited to stock up on the fruits of the Spirit? No wacky costumes necessary. As you grow in Jesus, you'll be like a strong, beautiful tree bearing lots of spiritual fruit you can share with others—all over town and beyond.

And that's a thought that is quite a-peeling (I'll stop now).

— ANDREW

WARNING: BUMPY ROAD AHEAD

"I have told you these things, so that in me you may have peace. In this world you will have trouble. But take heart! I have overcome the world."

—JOHN 16:33 NIV

We've taken many wild road trips during our YouTube career, but we've never done anything like the time we traveled the "highway of frozen death." Sounds ominous, right? Well, it was!

The highway of frozen death is the nickname given to Mosquito Pass, one of the highest-elevation roads in Colorado. The route climbs more than thirteen thousand feet into the cold Colorado air with steep grades and narrow paths. As if that weren't enough, the pass is often covered in snow and ice. In other words, it was the perfect place to film a video!

Our mission? To reach the pinnacle of Mosquito Pass, spend the night, and survive to tell the tale! To make this harrowing journey, we rented the most indestructible truck we could find—a thirteen-foot-high behemoth with tires higher than your waist.

Yet even with our monster vehicle, the trip was really difficult. It was a super-steep climb, and at one point, we had to move a boulder off the road just to keep driving. With the vehicle's stiff brakes, it felt like I was going to pull a quad muscle anytime we had to stop.

Although we thought about turning around many times, we pushed through and made it to the top. It was so rewarding! The views were incredible, and the feeling of accomplishment was insane.

In your life, there will be moments when the road feels too hard and the obstacles too great. What will you do? Will you give up, or will you find a way to push forward? A bumpy—even scary—path that feels impossible to travel is absolutely possible with Jesus.

Jesus never said life would be easy. In John 16:33, He promised that our paths will often be challenging. But remember, Jesus has overcome greater obstacles than we can ever imagine. And He promises His strength to all who follow Him.

Your obstacles might be physical, such as an illness or a disability. They could be mental or emotional challenges from a traumatic experience. They could be people who mock you for your faith or hurt you without reason. And there will certainly be spiritual obstacles too. God's enemy, Satan, does not want you to succeed.

So when you reach that huge boulder in the road, don't turn around. Ask for Jesus' strength to overcome it. Jesus has conquered, and with His help so can you! He is faithful, and the rewards are well worth it when you make it to the top.

—ANDREW

SHOW AND TELL

> Therefore, we are ambassadors for Christ, God
> making his appeal through us. We implore you
> on behalf of Christ, be reconciled to God.
> —2 CORINTHIANS 5:20

Every YouTuber starts small. But I vividly recall our first taste of fame when some well-known people shared our videos.

Back then, when we had fewer than 100,000 subscribers, our video "Falling Is the New Cone-ing" went viral. In the video, we purposely fell near people and got some great reactions.

As the video gained momentum, celebrities started taking notice, which was really exciting. Famous personalities shared the video on social media, and it even caught the attention of folks at Nickelodeon. It was a surreal experience, and we reveled in the knowledge that so many people were enjoying our content.

Yet as thrilling as *that* was, we get even more excited about sharing Jesus' offer of salvation. We are God's ambassadors—His representatives here on earth. It's our job to share how God transforms our hearts and welcomes us into the kingdom of God. We can't help telling others how God is changing us from the inside out. God has given us the unique privilege of inviting others into His kingdom. What an incredible honor!

When you share the good news of Jesus with others, there's

no pressure to make someone else believe. We don't change people's hearts; God does. Our job is simply to share what He's done in our lives because we genuinely want them to experience that kind of transformation too.

So be on the lookout for opportunities to share your faith. An ambassador represents the king and spreads his message far and wide. Share your personal story of what God has done in your life, and watch how the King of heaven uses your faithfulness as His ambassador to welcome others into His eternal kingdom!

It's fun when you learn that celebrities are sharing your social media content. But this news is fleeting—here one day, gone the next. The gospel of Jesus Christ is good news that changes lives forever.

— JUSTIN

WE DON'T CHANGE PEOPLE'S HEARTS; GOD DOES.

A FRUITFUL SCAVENGER HUNT

Grab a *bunch* of friends and practice the fruits of the Spirit (love, joy, peace, patience, kindness, goodness, faithfulness, gentleness, and self-control) on other shoppers and employees as you race through the grocery store on this mission to be fruit-filled! Trust us—you'll love this *berry* much.

RULES

1. Teams will have two or three people.
2. Each team needs a smartphone.
3. Teams have thirty minutes to complete the list.
4. The team must show a photo of the item to be counted.
5. An item must be fruit-themed (an actual fruit, made from fruit, fruit-flavored, or fruit-shaped).
6. The first team to return to the designated finish spot with all items found wins.
7. If no team finds all items, the team with the most items wins. If there's a tie, the team that finished first wins.
8. You can't use the same item twice.
9. You can't use an actual fruit for a "flavored" item.
10. Items must be actual products, not photos of products.
11. Feel free to award a prize—or simply let the winner walk away feeling like one in a *melon*.

ITEM CHECKLIST

- ☐ 1 pound of grapes (on a scale)
- ☐ something sour
- ☐ something orange
- ☐ something soft
- ☐ a mango
- ☐ something you've never eaten
- ☐ something an unexpected color
- ☐ something with seeds inside
- ☐ something in a bunch
- ☐ something crunchy
- ☐ something berry-flavored
- ☐ something that tastes nasty to you
- ☐ something that tickles
- ☐ a combination of three or more fruits
- ☐ something apple-flavored
- ☐ something banana-flavored
- ☐ tomatillo
- ☐ something soft
- ☐ something in a box
- ☐ something in a bag
- ☐ something cold
- ☐ something that grows on trees
- ☐ something you eat with a spoon
- ☐ a melon
- ☐ something under $1
- ☐ something over $5
- ☐ pizza topped with fruit
- ☐ meat
- ☐ something you can balance on your head (balanced on someone's head)
- ☐ something you can use to build a pyramid (in a pyramid)

Pro tip: Show kindness to the store workers, don't be wild, and return everything in good condition to its place after your photo.

Next level: Choose five items from the list to purchase and bring them home to create an original smoothie or snack.

TIME WELL SPENT

> **Seek the LORD and his strength; seek his presence continually!**
> —1 CHRONICLES 16:11

Making quality YouTube videos is a process! When we have an idea for a video, the final product is at the forefront of our minds. But a lot of work and time is involved to get there.

For most videos, we spend a couple hours crafting the idea and storyline. Then filming typically lasts two to four days. After that, the editors take over, and depending on the amount of footage involved, the post-production process usually takes another week or two. So every ten- to twenty-minute JStu video you enjoy on YouTube is the result of at least three weeks of work. And big ideas take even longer!

The same is true for our relationship with God. In order to become the God-follower you want to be, you have to put in time and effort.

Being a Christian is not just a label you wear. It's a personal relationship with God. You can't build a relationship with someone without spending time with them. Think about it: what's the difference between a friend and a complete stranger? You've spent way more time with your friend and zero time with that stranger! Your relationship with God works the same way. God will be a stranger to you if you never spend time with Him, but the more time you hang out in His presence, the closer you'll become to Him.

How do you do this with an invisible God who rules over heaven and earth? He's actually made it quite easy! We spend time with God by reading the Bible, thinking about what it says, and talking to Him in prayer.

Yes, God is big and huge and we can't see Him. But every second of our lives, He's near and personal! His Spirit lives inside every believer. He wants us to seek Him, and He's given us full access to His presence through His Son, Jesus.

A lot of people make excuses that they don't have enough time for quiet moments alone with God. Don't fall into this trap! The truth is, you *always* have time for what's most important to you. So prioritize time with God. It's time well spent, and the spiritual benefits are out of this world!

—ANDREW

IN ORDER TO BECOME THE GOD-FOLLOWER YOU WANT TO BE, YOU HAVE TO PUT IN TIME AND EFFORT.

THE GREATEST LOVE LETTER

"I have loved you with an everlasting love; therefore I have continued my faithfulness to you."
—JEREMIAH 31:3

In high school, my now-wife and I were masters at passing notes between classes. Rather than paying attention in class, I crafted romantic masterpieces (or so I told myself!).

Our notes were filled with drawings, inside jokes, and a secret code known only to us, and they created an excitement that still warms my heart. While the memories may induce a slight cringe at our silly teenage expressions of love, that time remains a cherished memory. And the connection those notes sparked holds strong to this day.

God has also written us a love letter, and thankfully it's far beyond the cheesy awkwardness of teen love notes! His letter is a true masterpiece, filled with reminders of His immeasurable love and kindness toward us. This love letter, of course, is the Bible.

The Bible—a big collection of sixty-six smaller books—tells one great story of God's saving love. The Bible is a divine work of art straight from God's heart. Through the history, poetry, sermons, and prophecies, you can always find the story of God's lavish affection for you. And while the Bible is for everyone, you can sometimes hear God speak directly to your heart through the

Holy Spirit when you read it. I love it when that happens! That's because God, as the all-knowing, all-powerful Author of life, knows you intimately and longs for you to know Him.

As I've grown in my faith, the Bible has changed my life. It's been a central part of growing my relationship with God and my relationships with others. To know that my Creator has shared His heart with me and wants to communicate with me is simply amazing.

I encourage you to dive deeper into the Bible. If you find it hard to understand, get a study Bible with helpful notes, join a Bible study group, attend a youth group, and ask lots of questions. Soon you'll be able to open His love letter to you with anticipation and expectation. As you immerse yourself in the Bible's truth, you'll experience a love like no other—a perfect love that transforms every aspect of your being. It's a love that stays with you through the highs and lows, a constant companion on your journey.

So open that love letter today. And tomorrow. And the next day. Read what God has penned just for you, and let it become your guiding light. Embrace the gift of His love, and let His Word continuously shape you for the better. His love is the greatest gift you'll ever receive, and it's waiting for you on every page.

—JUSTIN

INSPIRED

> **All Scripture is breathed out by God and profitable for teaching, for reproof, for correction, and for training in righteousness, that the man of God may be complete, equipped for every good work.**
> —2 TIMOTHY 3:16–17

In our business, inspiration is everything. Most of our videos were inspired by something we saw or heard somewhere else or something we personally experienced.

The inspiration for our earliest prank videos often came from really random stuff. One time, Justin was coming home from class and saw this little kid wearing squeaker shoes. With every step, this kid's shoes would make a noise. So naturally, Justin thought, *What if we had adult versions and walked around the library in them?* Wouldn't that be your first thought too? Needless to say, the idea of mixing a quiet library with an adult wearing squeaker shoes produced a great video.

Another inspiration was the classic "coin behind the ear" trick that magicians often use. We took that simple sleight-of-hand gag to the extreme and pulled random funny objects out of people's hair—things like toilet paper, pizzas, and fruit. (A magician never reveals his secrets, so you'll just have to watch the video to see how we did it!)

Inspiration is critical to the creative process. Every writer, painter, sculptor, musical composer, or other creator finds inspiration in the world around them. But without question, the ultimate inspiration award goes to the Bible! That's because the Bible—the greatest created work of all time—was inspired by God Himself.

SQUEEEAK!

From Genesis to Revelation, the Bible's sixty-six books were written by roughly forty different human authors over a span of more than one thousand years. Yet incredibly, all the books of the Bible form one story: how God has worked throughout history to save sinners like us through His Son, Jesus Christ.

How can forty people write different books that connect to one story? Because every word of Scripture was directly inspired by God. Second Timothy 3:16 describes this process as being "God-breathed." In other words, each biblical author wrote in their own style and era while God's Spirit prompted and directed them (see also 2 Peter 1:20–21).

Because of this heavenly inspiration, the Bible is just as relevant today as it was thousands of years ago. God is alive and so are all His words (Hebrews 4:12). The Bible's truth—cover to cover—is new and fresh for you today and every day. That's an inspiring thought indeed!

— ANDREW

LIGHTING THE WAY

Your word is a lamp to my feet and a light to my path.
—PSALM 119:105

Each week, we get bombarded with questions from awesome fans like you. Some of the common questions include "Are Justin and Andrew secret brothers?" and "How much cash are you raking in?"

Now, we can't spill all the tea because some things are top-secret and other answers are just a quick Google search away. (Although to be clear, no, Andrew and I aren't brothers.) But we get it—you're curious! You want to uncover the mysteries of who we are and what makes our YouTube channel tick. And we love that about you.

Life is full of questions and unknowns. Is it just me, or do you ever feel like you're living out a real-life choose-your-own-adventure book? It's easy to feel lost in the twists and turns. But fear not, my friend, because Psalm 119:105 points us to a super-important truth: God's Word is a perfect light to illuminate your way. The Bible is the ultimate flashlight that will brighten your path. It's better than any smartphone app or GPS device out there.

When you hit a fork in the road of life and you're standing there scratching your head, wondering which way to go, turn to the Bible. While it won't tell you every single decision you need to make, it *will* equip you with godly wisdom and faith to take the next step. The journey of faith is trusting God as you head into the unknown.

Sometimes Scripture will be very clear in its directions: "Don't lie," "don't steal," "love your enemies," "treasure God, not money." But other times, you'll need to take the Bible's guiding principles and pray for God's wisdom on how to proceed. These moments will strengthen your faith and add a splash of confidence to your journey as you see God's powerful guiding hand leading you every step of the way through both failures and successes.

So the next time you've got a question or you're stuck at a crossroads, open your Bible and turn on God's illuminating light. Soak in His wisdom and learn more about Jesus because life's adventures are best faced with a heavenly Friend by your side— One who has experienced real life with all its potholes and detours (Hebrews 4:15).

God has given you His Word for your good. Let Scripture light your way, and marvel at how life's questions start to become clearer.

— JUSTIN

FAITH IS TRUSTING GOD AS YOU HEAD INTO THE UNKNOWN.

HIDDEN IN THE HEART

I have stored up your word in my heart,
that I might not sin against you.
—PSALM 119:11

Have you ever read any of the following literary classics?

Bug Detective

Green Sisters

Where Do Camels Belong?

Neither have we.

These were a few of the books we recommended to complete strangers in the library during one of our prank videos. Since we hadn't read any of these books, we made up what they were about based on the title. Most people looked at us in confusion. Some declined our advice. And a few even said they might check the books out! Of course, they were probably just trying to be nice.

There are millions of books in the world, and many of them are pretty wacky. It's probably not the best idea to recommend weird books to strangers (unless it's for a YouTube video!). But there's one book I recommend to you above all others: the Bible!

When we read and treasure God's Word, we draw closer to the God who loves us, saves us, and calls us to follow Him. Memorizing Scripture helps us to grow more familiar with God. We get to know what He expects of us as His children so that we "might not sin against" Him. Plus, when you study Scripture, you'll receive amazing, practical benefits in your life! It'll help you . . .

- know your Creator and understand His purpose in creating you;
- understand how God saved you through His Son, Jesus;
- understand how God expects you to live;
- learn how to treat others with the love and humility Jesus had;
- learn how to navigate life's challenges;
- and much more!

Here's another cool thing: memorizing Scripture will help you stay on the right path even when decisions seem difficult or unclear. You'll have godly guiding principles to help you navigate even the trickiest challenges and hardest temptations. Don't let the world make choices for you. Look to God's Word!

As you study Scripture, God will begin to change your life day by day. You'll become more like Him as you grow in faith and wisdom. And that's something that won't ever happen with *Bug Detective* or *Where Do Camels Belong?*

—ANDREW

UNBREAKABLE

> "Heaven and earth will pass away, but
> my words will not pass away."
> —MATTHEW 24:35

The word *unbreakable* is pretty popular on YouTube. Whether the object in question is actually unbreakable or not, it's entertaining to see someone struggle to break the object.

We've done a few unbreakable videos on our channel. One of them was a treehouse. Our build team fortified a multilevel treehouse to the extreme, and my challenge was to break out of it. Our builders are really good at this stuff, so it was quite a workout to escape! I had to deal with thick floors, sticky glue that hindered my mobility, and a concrete door! It took a ridiculous amount of energy and effort—including pounding my way through concrete with a sledgehammer!—but after several hours, I finally broke free.

That treehouse was a beast, but it wasn't truly unbreakable. Nothing in this world is. Everything on earth will one day pass away—no matter how thick the structure is, what it's made of, or how well it's built. In fact, as Matthew 24:35 says, even the universe itself won't last forever.

But God's Word will.

The lasting power of Scripture is unlike anything else in creation. It's one of the most amazing things about God's Word, and it's why you can put your full trust in the Bible.

In the "unbreakable" treehouse, I was able to slowly chip away at the structure until I created a hole large enough to escape through. After that, the treehouse wasn't useable anymore, so we threw it away. This will be the fate of everything in the uni-verse when Jesus returns. Once the old is gone, He will create "new heavens and a new earth" (Isaiah 65:17) that will last forever.

The truth of Scripture cannot be destroyed. You can't chip away at it, erase it, or shatter it. God's Word is eternal, and His promises will endure because they come directly from the Source of all truth, wisdom, and power.

Every word Jesus utters, every truth He speaks, every prom-ise He and God make throughout Scripture—all of it will come to pass. It's true yesterday, today, and forever.

So the next time you watch an "unbreakable" video or you accidentally drop your mom's fine china or you fracture your wrist while skateboarding, remember this verse. Everything else in life is breakable and will fade away. But God's Word will last forever.

—ANDREW

CRITICAL CONVOS

"When you pray, go into your room and shut the door and pray to your Father who is in secret. And your Father who sees in secret will reward you."
—MATTHEW 6:6

Have you ever caught yourself having a full-on conversation with . . . yourself? Guilty as charged!

In one of our early prank videos, we pretended to be in conversation with total strangers. Earbuds in and sunglasses on, we'd stand next to people and start talking, making them think we were in deep conversation with them.

After some funny banter, we'd remove our earbuds and say, "Oh, I'm sorry. I was on the phone. Were you talking to me?" The reactions were hilarious.

We've all had goofy conversations before, from these kinds of interactions to, as kids, the moments when we talked to our stuffed animals and had heart-to-hearts with LEGO figures. (Or maybe that was just me.)

There's nothing wrong with a little solo chitchat, but that will only get you so far. We all need someone to talk to, and there's no one greater to connect with than our heavenly Father. Prayer is simply talking to God—and it's an incredible gift. The Creator and Ruler of the universe wants to hear from us, anytime and anywhere!

Our prank was all about mixed messages and bad communication, but when we pray, God hears us loud and clear. And our words don't land on deaf ears like when we spill our secrets to a teddy bear.

Prayer is an act of faith because it's communication with an invisible God. But it's also just a basic conversation. You can worship Him with some compliments, thank Him for being awesome and giving you good things, and ask Him for anything.

And God answers! His responses might not always match our wish list, but that's because He's got the ultimate game plan. God opens and closes doors according to His master plan, and praying is our way of saying, *Okay, God, Your call.*

The convos we had with stuffed animals years ago weren't just a quirky habit; they were about genuinely connecting with our plush pals. In a far greater way, when we talk to God, it's about building a relationship with the living, all-powerful Creator of everything!

God doesn't pull a "talk to someone else" move like we did in our sneaky prank. He's all ears for us, listening to our hearts' desires with a love beyond comprehension.

So talk to God often. Believe that He's listening, trust in His perfect answers, and step into the unknown with faith. God is always just a prayer away!

— JUSTIN

HEAVENLY CONVERSATION STARTER

Pray then like this: "Our Father in heaven, hallowed be your name. Your kingdom come, your will be done, on earth as it is in heaven."
—MATTHEW 6:9–10

Years ago, we found an online tutorial video of a guy giving advice on how to start conversations. We thought the advice was really funny and unrealistic. So we tested it. Following his advice, we tried to start conversations with random strangers by using intros such as:

"Who's having the most fun in this place right now?"

"What's the name of this song playing?" (It's even funnier when there *isn't* a song playing!)

"This place is beautiful. Have you ever been here before?" (The reactions you get when saying this to a drive-thru employee are pretty great.)

"That drink looks amazing. What is that?" (Ask this of someone who's clearly drinking water!)

Sure enough, there were some very awkward moments in these convos! Starting conversations with people can be hard. But it doesn't have to be that way when we pray to God!

Out of His great love for us, the God of the universe has given us the privilege of talking to Him personally anytime, anywhere, no matter how we're feeling. He wants prayer to come naturally—and often—for us.

But sometimes it doesn't. Maybe that's why Jesus gave us an example of how to pray with the Lord's Prayer, found in Matthew 6:9–13.

Many people recite the Lord's Prayer, which is great. But you don't have to stop there! Jesus meant for that prayer to be a starting point—and a general pattern—to model our prayers after. The Lord's Prayer covers lots of different topics that you can dive deeper into in your own time with Him, such as worship, thankfulness, forgiveness, and making requests. As you grow in your prayer life, you'll grow in your relationship with God.

Thanks to the example of the Lord's Prayer, the ultimate conversation starter, you can feel confident in your communication with God. Just like in any other relationship, the more conversations you have with God, the easier it'll be in the future. And don't be nervous about doing it wrong. God knows your heart and your intentions. He wants to hear from you, even when you're awkward.

That conversation starter video was pretty goofy. But one of the tips does seem to fit well with today's topic: "There's something interesting about you. I just had to come meet you."

There's no one more interesting than God. Go meet Him in prayer today!

—ANDREW

FOLLOW THE LEADER

> "When the Spirit of truth comes, he will guide you into all the truth, for he will not speak on his own authority, but whatever he hears he will speak, and he will declare to you the things that are to come."
>
> —JOHN 16:13

The JStu team has looked different over the years, with people coming and going. One former member was Seth, nicknamed Hyper. You can probably guess how he got his nickname—his energy was off the charts!

Hyper moved with his wife from Texas to Colorado to join our team, and it was a great fit. We created tons of fun videos together, and he quickly became a fan favorite.

But life has a funny way of changing. As Hyper and his wife were thinking about starting a family, he sensed the Holy Spirit leading them back to Texas. Back in Texas they'd be closer to their families, and Hyper could work as the youth pastor at his dad's church. After spending a lot of time reading the Bible and praying about moving, Hyper knew that returning to Texas was the right thing to do. His departure was a bittersweet moment for the JStu team. But we knew he was making a good decision, and we were happy for him.

Life is full of choices—some big, some small. But how do we

know what choices to make? I have good news: God hasn't left us to fend for ourselves! He has given us the Holy Spirit to guide us.

The Holy Spirit is part of the Trinity. He is fully God, just like God the Father and God the Son (Jesus). God sends His Spirit to live inside every believer who puts their faith in Jesus. Amazing!

It's vital for Christians to follow the Holy Spirit's guidance. But how can you recognize His leading?

The first step is to read the Bible often. God's Spirit speaks through His Word, and He will use your time in Scripture to prompt your heart in certain directions. Second, pray often. Prayer is like a DM to heaven! And even when you don't know what to say, the Spirit speaks to the Father on your behalf (Romans 8:27). Wow!

As you keep seeking the Lord through His Word and prayer, the Spirit will nudge you in certain directions. He'll open and close doors. He'll also bring wise advice from godly people into your life. The Holy Spirit speaks through all these ways.

It takes time to learn how to hear the Holy Spirit's guidance, so don't be discouraged if it feels a bit mysterious at first. God is faithful. His Spirit will always be with you as a ready guide.

—ANDREW

BETTER TOGETHER

> Let us consider how to stir up one another to love and good works, not neglecting to meet together, as is the habit of some, but encouraging one another, and all the more as you see the Day drawing near.
> —HEBREWS 10:24–25

While Andrew and I are in most of our JStu videos, sometimes you'll catch other team members joining our adventures. And trust me, it's always a blast. Multiple personalities, lots of energy . . . what could possibly go wrong?

For one video, five of us embarked on a hilarious overnight quest in a microhotel—the key term being *micro*—we built just for the occasion. Some of the rooms weren't even big enough for a kid-size bed, and our friend Blake got stuck in a room with nothing more than a pet cushion to sleep on. I love these experiences. They're fun and unique, but they also deepen the bonds I have with my friends.

Quality friendships are an absolute must in life, and this is no different when you're a follower of Jesus. The importance of godly friendships and fellowship within the community of believers can't be overstated.

Being part of a Christian community is crucial for your spiritual growth. God wants His children to spend time together regularly so we can strengthen one another's faith. You can't learn from others and encourage each other if you're never near them. Sure, we all need our alone time, but living as a lone wolf all the time doesn't work. We all need some community.

Gathering together with other believers creates opportunities for our faith to be sharpened. We can learn from each other's successes and failures, witnessing how God moves in each other's lives.

So take a moment today to reflect on what your Christian community looks like. Do you spend time with others who are trying to follow Jesus, reading God's Word, and acting in ways that honor Him? It's a vital aspect of your life that will significantly impact your faith, just as it did for me.

And don't worry—no one's going to make you sleep on a pet cushion.

— JUSTIN

CHILL SPOT

Spending time in prayer and in God's Word are a regular part of a Jesus follower's life. So let's do it in style! Create a space in your bedroom or other quiet place in your home where you can spend time with God and chill.

Start your spot by building a cozy canopy.

SUPPLIES

one Command Curtain Rod Hook or a nail and hammer
three or four pieces of long, wide fabric (at least 8 feet long and 3 feet wide)
rubber band
piece of string, cut to 1 foot long
seating option(s):

- single or twin mattress with fitted sheet
- oversized pillows
- beanbag
- chair

five to ten strands
    of string
    lights
extra pillows and
    blanket

INSTRUCTIONS

1. About six feet off the floor, affix a nail or Command Curtain Rod Hook into the wall.
2. Bring the ends of the fabric pieces together. Wrap a rubber band around the ends, with several inches of material hanging above the band.
3. Thread the string through the rubber band and tie to form a loop.
4. Use the loop to hang the curtain from the hook or nail.
5. Place your seating option below the hanging curtains.
6. Drape the curtains around the seat, or tuck them underneath the edges of a mattress or pillow.
7. Hang string lights from the hook or nail, and drape the lights down the curtains. Plug the lights into a wall outlet.
8. Add additional pillows and blankets to send the cozy meter off the charts!

Next level: Add any of the following options:

- a colorful sign featuring your chill spot's nickname
- a bookshelf
- fake or real potted plants
- wall art
- a container of snacks
- a reading lamp

REPPIN' THE NAME

> Therefore, as God's chosen people, holy and
> dearly loved, clothe yourselves with compassion,
> kindness, humility, gentleness and patience.
> —COLOSSIANS 3:12 NIV

I've lost track of the number of costumes we've worn since starting our YouTube journey in 2011. We've pretended to be superheroes, safari hunters, military personnel, elderly folks, and much more. For one video, we hit the same fast-food drive-thru fifty times as fifty different characters! That's a ton of costumes—not to mention a frightening amount of greasy food.

There's just something so fun about stepping into another persona, even if it's just for a goofy video. Putting on a costume is more than just a change of clothes; it's diving into the essence of that character—the accent, the mannerisms, everything! The more we embody that character, the better the video turns out.

If you're serious about following God, you need to embrace the essence of who He created you to be. The Bible tells us that God made us in His image. That doesn't mean we're mini gods. Being made in God's image means God crafted us to reflect His attributes, reveal His character, and embody His goodness for others around us.

While we're like God in many ways (we can think, speak, plan, create, feel emotions, and more), we're certainly not like Him in *every* way! We sin; He's holy. We know a little; He knows everything. Our bench press isn't very impressive; He is all-powerful. But unlike anything else in creation, we *do* bear the image of our Creator!

Living as God's image-bearer isn't an act we perform in Christian circles or a costume we wear at church on Sundays and throw aside the rest of the week. It's part of our core being. It's who we are, and it kicks into high gear when we trust in Jesus as our Savior.

God designed you to mirror Him in incredible ways. And as we become more like Him day by day, we can genuinely walk in His likeness. Love, joy, peace, patience, and all the other fruits of the Spirit—these aren't costumes we wear. They're the characteristics of who we are in Jesus!

Remember, you are God's image-bearer. You're no longer bound to the "costume" of your old self. You've put on wonderful newness of being a child of God. So embrace your high calling and represent Him well!

— JUSTIN

KNOWN BY GOD

For the eyes of the Lord are on the righteous, and his ears are open to their prayer. But the face of the Lord is against those who do evil.
—1 PETER 3:12

This amazing experience happens from time to time: we run into our incredible fans. Whether it's in our favorite store, at a trampoline park, or in a restaurant, meeting our fans is always a blast. We love seeing the vibrant enthusiasm from people who support our goofy YouTube adventures and genuinely love what we do. It's an encouragement that fuels our passion.

Our fans seem to know everything about us. They've followed our journey and watched hours of our mischief. It feels like we're old friends to them. On the flip side, we don't know them at all. All we know is their name and that they really dig our budget challenges!

What if your favorite celebrity ran into you and knew exactly who you were? You'd feel pretty awesome! That's exactly what happens with God. He's the coolest celebrity in the universe, and He's your biggest fan. He knows everything about you and still loves you like crazy. He intentionally and uniquely created you, and He knows you better than anyone else ever could. His heart beats for you!

Let that reality sink in. The One who created the universe didn't just peace out when He was done creating. He knows you by name, and He desires a deep, personal relationship with you.

He's super psyched about everything you're up to and wants to take you on epic adventures.

If you are a follower of Jesus, God isn't your fan. He's your Father. A Father who created and rules the entire universe. A Father who possesses all knowledge, wisdom, and power. A Father who makes zero mistakes. A Father who loves you more than you can imagine. Believing this truth can truly change your life; I know it did for me.

So whether or not we ever meet you in person, remember this: if you trust in God, His caring eyes are upon you and His ears hear every word you tell Him. Far from being a mere spectator, He's your loving Father who knows you and loves you perfectly in every way.

— JUSTIN

BELIEVE THAT GOD IS YOUR LOVING FATHER. IT WILL CHANGE YOUR LIFE.

YOU BELONG HERE

God sent forth his Son, born of woman, born under the law, to redeem those who were under the law, so that we might receive adoption as sons. And because you are sons, God has sent the Spirit of his Son into our hearts, crying, "Abba! Father!"
—GALATIANS 4:4–6

A few years ago, my in-laws decided to adopt a little boy named Jeremy. They specifically chose to make Jeremy their child. They brought him home and gave him everything a little boy needs: clothes, a cozy bed, toys, and lots and lots of love. He's now their son, just the same as their other kiddos.

Some human parents who adopt look for a certain type of child. They might want a boy or a girl, a child from a specific country or of a certain age. If they are adopting an older child, they might even want someone who is interested in sports or art or building. It's a wonderful thing to be chosen!

Human adoption is a beautiful picture of the way God chooses to bring people into His family. But God doesn't have a list of criteria to be His child. And He doesn't choose just one or even a few children. God is always looking to build His family bigger. He wants everyone—no matter who we are, what we look like, or where we're from—to become His children by following His Son, Jesus.

Because of our sinful nature, each of us was born separated from God (Romans 5:12). But out of His great love and mercy, God has chosen to adopt countless children into His heavenly family. Through Jesus, God becomes our "Abba Father." *Abba* is an ancient Aramaic word that basically means "Daddy." God loves you with a love so huge that it's larger than the heart-bursting emotion of a dad holding his newborn or hugging his newly adopted child for the first time.

Everything an earthly father can do, God can do better—*way* better! He'll always be there when you get in trouble and need help. He'll give the right advice every time. He'll love you no matter how many mistakes you make. And He doesn't care if you win the game, get straight As, or can bench-press your own weight. He'll love you the same when you're a teenager as He did when you were a tiny baby. And He'll think you're adorable when you have gray hair.

When we trust in Jesus as our Lord and Savior, God adopts us into His family as His children. He's our perfect Daddy now on earth and forever in heaven.

Families on earth have limits. My in-laws have eight children, including Jeremy. That's a lot of kids! But God's heavenly family has no space limits. He has room for you too.

Are you part of the fam?

—ANDREW

GOD DOESN'T HAVE A LIST OF CRITERIA TO BE HIS CHILD.

ONE OF A KIND

You formed my inward parts; you knitted me
together in my mother's womb. I praise you,
for I am fearfully and wonderfully made.
—PSALM 139:13–14

I love sports trading cards. There's something really fun about opening a new pack of cards to see what treasures await inside. And if you get a superstar's rookie card or another rare card . . . *CHA-CHING*! You hit the jackpot!

Many sports trading cards these days have rarity values on them. For example, if a card features an engraving that shows *40/100*, it means there are only one hundred of that specific card ever made and you got the fortieth one. Pretty cool! The rarest and most expensive cards, of course, say *1/1*. If you get *that* kind of card—well, hot diggity dog! You just found an incredibly rare collectible, a card that is truly one of a kind. Because there is only one, the value for that card is higher than any other card.

When God designed you, He made you a 1/1. You are a rarity. You are invaluable. Your worth is beyond measure. There are more than eight billion people on planet earth right now, yet there's no one exactly like you in the whole world. And God designed it that way!

I see this dynamic at work on the JStu team every day. Each

person has their own unique skills, interests, and personality traits. Blake, for example, is quiet and reserved. But he's also the funniest person on the team. His timing and responses can make anyone laugh. Rick is an extremely hard worker. And if you ask him anything about cars or LEGO, his eyes light up like a Christmas tree. Samuel is a great teacher

and leader; he can be very expressive too. If you tell him something interesting, he'll likely respond, "Oh, wooowww!"

God fearfully and wonderfully made each person on our team, and He did the same with you. He created you with love, intention, and great detail to make someone new, someone different from every other human He has ever created. The way He designed your hair color, eyes, height, personality, facial expressions, laughter, and smile—all of it shows you truly are one of a kind.

Satan will try to whisper lies about who you are. You'll hear the same from the world around you—a world already broken by Satan's lies. Don't believe any of it. Your individuality is special and invaluable. You are God's 1/1. A rarity. His masterpiece.

— ANDREW

PEOPLE PLEASER OR GOD PLEASER?

Am I now seeking the approval of man, or of God?
Or am I trying to please man? If I were still trying
to please man, I would not be a servant of Christ.
—GALATIANS 1:10

In today's highly digital world, it's harder than ever to avoid getting consumed by what other people think.

For us at JStu, running a business on social media can be tricky. The more views, likes, and comments we get, the more we know the content is doing well. That's a good feeling. But the opposite is also true. If a video doesn't get the feedback we were anticipating, it can be disappointing.

There's a balance here. As YouTubers, we want people who watch our videos and see our posts to enjoy them and respond accordingly. But it's tempting to focus solely on what people think. If we do that, we become people pleasers, being controlled by what others say and want. And that's a dangerous place to be.

When the apostle Paul wrote Galatians 1:10 back in the first century AD, he certainly wasn't referring to social media! But the truth he shared is timeless. We should focus our attention on serving God, not on pleasing others.

Our focus on YouTube is to make people laugh daily—that's our motto! And we do that while also making wholesome,

God-honoring content the whole family can watch. We don't always hit the mark because we're human, but that's the goal. When we keep our eyes focused on our God-first mission, everything else falls into its proper place.

What about you? Are you more focused on pleasing God or on pleasing the people around you? If you have any social media accounts, do you find yourself constantly looking at how many "friends" you have online and the amount of likes your posts get? Do you find yourself comparing these amounts to those on other people's pages?

This issue goes far beyond our online activity. The question of who we ultimately want to please is a matter of the heart. Whose praise do we care about most—God's or people's? The real desires of our heart will reveal themselves in our actions—online and elsewhere.

Human praise will never fully satisfy. But God's approval will last into eternity. So make it easier on yourself, and aim to please the One who created you! This isn't to earn God's favor. If you're a believer, He's already given that to you through Jesus and what Jesus accomplished on the cross. Instead, aim to please God as a way to express your love and obedience to Him.

You've already been given the most fulfilling "like" ever—God's unending love toward you through Jesus. That's worth more than all the social media followers in the world.

—ANDREW

REAL VS. FAKE

Deliver me, O Lord, from lying lips,
from a deceitful tongue.
—PSALM 120:2

Huge muscles. Every guy wants them, but few actually achieve them. Well, not to brag or anything, but years ago we got really buff—with the help of a couple massive muscle suits!

For our "Huge Muscles in Public" video, we put on fake muscle suits underneath our regular clothing. Then we visited a few different places around town. Whether it was curling dumbbells in front of girls at the library, trying to become "Bicep Brothers" with truly ripped guys at the gym, or asking someone if we could bench-press them, it was a real hoot! We looked absolutely ridiculous faking the level of strength that takes years to build up to.

This video highlights a valuable life lesson: Don't pretend to be something you're not. Instead, be the person God created you to be!

In a world filled with conflicting messages about personal image and identity, it's crucial to embrace the uniqueness God designed within you. If uniformity were the goal, God could have created a world filled with identical robots. Instead, He crafted diverse individuals with distinct purposes—like you!

God has extraordinary plans for your life—plans only you can fulfill. So resist the temptation to fake something that's not really you. Avoid the urge to look or act a certain way that clearly isn't how God designed you. Doing so insults the unique qualities God gave you for His glory and your good.

Authenticity is a good thing. Being the person God created you to be honors Him. So rejoice that you are fearfully and wonderfully made, designed with a purpose meant only for you! Your unique identity—how you look, your personality, your interests and abilities—is all a testament to God's creativity.

Being authentic is also important for building real relationships with others. People can usually sniff out a fake. Just like we couldn't truly trick anyone with our fake-muscle costumes, you can't build authentic friendships if you're pretending to be someone else.

If you really want to imitate others, follow the godly characterics you see in mature Christians—things such as love, patience, generosity, and humility.

Above all, be yourself. Keep leaning into the person God created you to be while ultimately striving to be more like Jesus.

Now *that's* someone to imitate!

—JUSTIN AND ANDREW

WHAT MAKES YOU TICK?

Having gifts that differ according to the grace given to us, let us use them.
—ROMANS 12:6

Justin and I love hamming it up together in our YouTube videos and other JStu material. We've been great friends for a long time, and we share a lot of the same interests, thoughts, and humor.

But we also have many differences. For instance, Justin is much more outgoing than I am. He can create connections with almost anyone, which has helped our channel a lot. Justin's gifts fill in the gaps where I'm not as talented and vice versa. It's a really cool setup that only God could have planned.

And that's just the two of us. We have an entire team of amazing people who bring their own unique talents and interests to JStu! Take Rick, for instance. He's one of the most talented artists I know. He blows my mind with his ability to draw a portrait of someone in pencil and make it look like a real photo.

Then there's Drew and his harmonica. Now, most of us have blown into a toy harmonica before, and the result is usually a disturbing mixture of off-key tunes and flying slobber. But Drew is a legit harmonica whiz! He plays real songs, and they sound great. Those are just a few examples from our very talented team.

God has given every person—including you!—unique talents.

He gives these abilities to us out of His grace—aka His undeserved love and favor toward us—so that we can use them for His glory and the good of others.

God didn't create us to live on an island; He made us for community. He gives people different gifts because He wants us to work together. We can build His kingdom by using our talents to encourage other believers and to show Jesus to people who need to hear about Him. Even if you have the same talents as someone else, you'll likely use them in different ways and impact different people.

So what makes you tick? Whatever you're good at, use those talents to benefit people around you and serve the Lord. You might not be a great artist, and you might slobber a little too much when you play the harmonica, but you are a talented child of God. So get out there and use your talents for His glory!

—ANDREW

GOD GIVES BELIEVERS SPECIAL GIFTS FOR GLORIFYING HIM THAT WE CALL *SPIRITUAL GIFTS*. READ ABOUT THESE IN ROMANS 12:3-8, 1 CORINTHIANS 12, AND 1 PETER 4:10-11.

GLOW-UP

As for you, O man of God, flee these
things. Pursue righteousness, godliness,
faith, love, steadfastness, gentleness.
—1 TIMOTHY 6:11

Most folks know us at JStu for our wild challenges and adventures on our YouTube channel. But here's a little secret: we also dabble in making music!

Over the years, we've been blessed to collaborate with some incredibly talented people to record songs. One of my personal favorites is called "You Changed," written by our friend Seth (Remember "Hyper"?). The song talks about the change every Christian goes through on their journey of pursuing godliness.

Change is a big topic these days. Whether it's fitness routines, fashion advice, a reading challenge, or other "solutions," there are endless self-improvement plans out there. But the greatest self-improvement plan you can ever go on is growing in godliness, a process that is spiritual and unseen.

Each of us starts life separated from God and lost in our sins. But when we experience the transformation of being made new through Jesus, something changes inside us. As followers of Jesus, God calls us to throw away the sins of our past and chase after goodness. The real game-changer is the Holy Spirit, our ultimate life coach and personal trainer. Day by day, He whittles away our old desires and shapes us more into the image of Jesus.

The Bible says change is essential for the Christian life. To be a Christian, you need to change from the sinful person you were before God intervened to the righteous person He wants you to become. You need to make good choices that honor God. Toxic habits? Out the window. Keeping anger in check? Absolutely. Prioritizing good friendships? A big deal. These are just a few examples of the transformations that should accompany your commitment to God.

In my own journey, I used to feel trapped in shame, unable to break free from the cycle of sin. But then Jesus came into my life, giving me the power to overcome temptation. Christians certainly aren't perfect. We'll mess up more than we'd prefer. But as we seek God's forgiveness, He gives us grace and continues to transform us into the image of His Son.

So if you've encountered Jesus, take a moment and think about the ways you've changed—and the ways you still need to improve. Acknowledge the incredible grace God has showered on you as He's guided you every step of the way. Remember, He'll never leave or forsake you. If the world says you're uncool because of the differences in your life or if the devil attempts to pull you back into your old ways, don't buy into it.

In Christ, you've changed. And that's good news!

—JUSTIN

WONDERFULLY CREATED

So God created man in his own image, in the image of God he created him; male and female he created them.

—GENESIS 1:27

When my children were born, I experienced some of the most incredible and joyous moments of my life. (Talk about an adrenaline rush!) My wife and I were so excited to welcome them into our family and teach them all about Jesus, their identity, and what it means to be a Christ follower.

I love being a dad, like really, really love it. But you know who is the ultimate dad? Our Heavenly Father. And He loves being a dad to all of us. I mean, think about it. He created you and me with so much care and intentionality! Whether you're a boy or girl, God loves you and created you with a specific purpose. And each of us have unique qualities that contribute to the beauty of God's creation. That's right! God doesn't just love what you like about yourself. He loves all of you because He created and designed you to be just as you are!

I was in awe when I held my son and daughter for the first time. Each child is a distinct creation, reflecting the intentional diversity of God's design. Seeing God's specific handiwork—which was apparent in each of my babies even in those first moments—was a beautiful thing.

Want to know something even cooler? In Genesis 1, the first chapter in Scripture, the Bible says that God created us as male and female in His image. That's right, God created you in HIS image! Talk about mind blowing. The King of kings—the ultimate Father—created you and me in His image. This is why being you and embracing who God made you to be is so important. He made you with purpose and a plan in mind, and He wants you to love yourself just as you are because He loves you just as you are.

Whether you are a boy or girl, short or tall, light haired or dark haired, introverted or extroverted . . . you are a beautiful expression of God's purpose for your life. Embrace who you are, praise God for His awesome creativity, and enjoy the extraordinary journey God designed just for you.

— JUSTIN

SPEAK TRUTH KINDLY

> Let your speech always be gracious,
> seasoned with salt, so that you may know
> how you ought to answer each person.
> —COLOSSIANS 4:6

Our world is constantly changing. Ask your grandparents about their childhood, and you'll notice some things are similar to what it's like to be your age now—kids have always liked candy and staying up *way* past their bedtimes! But some things are different. That's what happens when culture (aka the world we live in) decides something is okay now or something isn't okay anymore.

If you haven't already, someday you'll meet people who have different beliefs than you. They might've grown up in a different place from you. They might be from a different ethnic background. They might even have different religious beliefs than yours.

When you talk with people and learn that they believe things contrary to what the Bible says, the conversation can get tricky *real* fast. You don't want to make them mad. But you also want them to understand that what God says is true. That's why it's so important to approach these people and the conversations with them with wisdom, grace, and gentleness. Just like Jesus would.

The world may try to censor you or hate on you for standing up for what the Bible says. But don't fall for that trap. God's Word is truth, and you should never be ashamed of it. But as you take a stand for truth, it's also really important to show respect for others and show Jesus' humility.

Communicating with people whose views are different than yours is like preparing steak. For the best results, a cook first seasons and marinates the meat. Thoughtfulness and preparation make all the difference. A well-prepared steak is so much tastier than a slab of meat that's just thrown onto the grill. In the same way, put thoughtfulness, prayer, and preparation into your relationships with people who see the world differently. Jesus used this approach when He lived on earth, and it's what He calls us to do as His followers.

It's easy to point fingers at people whose choices are different from what God says is right. But that's not a helpful or God-honoring way to communicate. Jesus prioritized relationships—deep connections built on trust. He had plenty of conversations with people who disagreed with Him, but He always spoke the truth in love.

It's not your job to change everyone you disagree with. Be the friend who displays Jesus' love through your words and actions. Offer encouragement and prayer to those who are struggling with their identity or values, and allow God to work on their hearts.

Your words have the power to impact lives positively. Season them well. You can be an instrument of change, and your kindness might be the spark someone needs to draw closer to Jesus.

— JUSTIN

STYLIN' AND PROFILIN' COSTUME CHALLENGE

There's only one you in the whole world! But pretending to be someone or something else isn't *always* bad. Sometimes it's downright hilarious! At JStu, we've put on plenty of costumes and assumed other identities for our videos (our "Same Drive-Thru 50 Times as 50 Different Characters" and "Extreme Fashion Show Budget Challenge" videos come to mind!)

Now it's your turn! Are you ready for an epic costume challenge? Let's go!

RULES

1. Write character categories on strips of paper, and place them in a bowl. Take turns picking your character.
2. Gather costume pieces from around the house, a sibling's dress-up bin, Grandma's closet, etc. You can also create costume pieces with paper, cardboard, and fabric scraps.
3. When everyone is ready, take turns acting out your character. Each person has thirty seconds for their act.
4. After each contestant's turn, the other contestants give scores between one and ten (ten being the best).
5. The highest score wins! If there's a tie, the other contestants will award a new score based on the creativity of the costume. The most creative player is the stylin' superstar.

COSTUME CATEGORY IDEAS

- millionaire
- cowboy/Western
- music star
- Disney character
- military
- someone from the future
- movie or video game character
- superhero
- 1980s
- 1970s
- grandpa or grandma
- teacher

Next level: Wear the costumes in public: a youth group event, trip to the local mall, or out for pizza.

WISHFUL THINKING

Now hope that is seen is not hope. For who hopes for what he sees? But if we hope for what we do not see, we wait for it with patience.

—ROMANS 8:24–25

I remember the day we hit our first milestone of one hundred thousand YouTube channel subscribers and snagged a shiny YouTube award plaque. Back when we started the channel, the idea of reaching such a massive audience seemed like a far-off dream—even an impossibility. Now we're setting our sights on the next mega goal.

In our JStu journey, we've always set our gaze on new milestones. Hit one, celebrate, then dream up the next big thing. It's like a never-ending chase that keeps us on our toes. But these goals are more than just numbers. They give us a road map, a sense of direction, and something exciting to pursue.

Still, all our JStu dreams are human plans and desires—goals that might or might not come true. We sure want them to, but there's no guarantee.

But as followers of Jesus, we have a true and far greater hope: the hope of eternal life with our Savior. Unlike our JStu aspirations, the hope of heaven is a rock-solid, fully guaranteed promise that is sure to come true. How do we know? Because God promises it. And when God makes a promise, it always happens.

Here's the thing about hope: you can't see the end goal. We can't see God or heaven, but we know they're real—we have *faith* they're real. This is one of the most exciting, mysterious, and sometimes difficult parts of the Christian life! That's because we rely on our senses so much. If we can't see, hear, taste, touch, or smell something, we often have a hard time believing it to be real.

Yet God requires faith—believing without seeing—from all His children. As 2 Corinthians 5:7 says, "We walk by faith, not by sight."

Thankfully, one day our faith will become sight! We will taste the riches of God's never-ending goodness. We will hear the praise of mighty angelic armies. We will touch the risen Savior. And we will see God face-to-face. This is the confident, absolutely-coming-true expectation of every Christian.

So the next time you're discouraged and feel like the future is unclear, remember the truth of Romans 8:24–25. Yep, we have some waiting to do to reach the end goal. But our hope is not wishful thinking. One day, the hope of heaven will turn into reality for every follower of Jesus.

Guaranteed.

—JUSTIN

CHRISTMAS EVERY DAY!

**May the God of hope fill you with all joy and
peace in believing, so that by the power of
the Holy Spirit you may abound in hope.**
—ROMANS 15:13

Don't you *love* waking up on Christmas morning? As a kid—and to be honest, as an adult—I'm filled with the hope of getting the gift I asked for under the tree.

One particular Christmas during my childhood, I remember waking up with *big* hopes and plans. I'd asked for one of the really big LEGO sets, and I was going to build the day away. As my family opened the presents, I hopped around with excitement. But when all the paper had been torn off, the LEGO set hadn't been in any of the packages. I was so disappointed!

Another Christmas, my parents bought a foosball table for me and my brother. We were thrilled! We played it all the time and had tournaments when our friends came over. After a while, though, it got moved into the garage. We used it less and less, and eventually we stopped playing with it. After a year or so, my parents sold it. (Nowadays, I'm more into ping-pong anyway!)

That's how it usually goes with stuff. We want that one killer toy more than anything else . . . until we don't care that much. All we want to do is play with the new *best thing ever* . . . until it gets old. Material things end up losing their appeal. So why do we keep chasing and telling ourselves we need *that* thing to be happy?

You will never find lasting hope or joy in any *thing* here on earth. Because that stuff won't last beyond this life. Yet Christians can find joy that lasts. Because Jesus lives forever, everyone who trusts in Him can too. And everything He gives us—a peace-filled home in heaven, a loving relationship with Him today, along with our brothers and sisters in God's family and the promises of His Word—will never end.

Are you feeling hopeful yet?

God is the God of hope! He always gives what He promises and He never disappoints. Are you ready to ask for the best gift you'll ever receive? Are you ready for the gift that never fades or breaks or goes out of style? All you have to do is step out in faith and ask Jesus to be your Lord and Savior. And then all the promises of the Bible are yours for now and eternity.

Don't set your heart on material things making you happy. Hope in God! It's the gift that keeps on giving.

—ANDREW

GOD ALWAYS GIVES WHAT HE PROMISES.

PROMISE KEEPER

All of God's promises have been fulfilled in Christ with a resounding "Yes!"
—2 CORINTHIANS 1:20 NLT

Have you ever encountered the disappointment of a broken promise? I certainly have.

A while ago, Andrew and I decided to take a leap of faith and audition for our favorite reality show. We submitted an audition video and received an exhilarating email saying, "We would like to cast you guys for the next season!"

Our excitement levels were off the charts! But despite phone calls, signed contracts, and eager anticipation, our promise of being cast crumbled. They ended up choosing someone else instead. We were so bummed! But then we heard back again—it was on! Our emotions soared once again. But the same thing happened. Our dreams were crushed.

That experience was a major letdown. But you know who never lets us down? God. He always keeps His promises. What He says, He does—every. single. time.

Think about all the promises God made and kept in the Bible. He promised Noah that He'd never destroy the earth again with a cataclysmic flood. Promise kept. He promised Abraham to make a great nation from his descendants. Promise kept. He promised

Moses that He'd deliver Israel from Egyptian slavery and bring His people into the promised land. Promise kept. And those promises cover just the first few chapters of the Bible! There are so many more. The greatest promise He ever made was to provide salvation from our sins through Jesus.

Promise kept.

If you are His child through faith in Jesus, God has also made many promises to you! He promises to never leave you or forsake you. He promises to work all things—even the crummy stuff—for your good. He promises hope, joy, peace, and eternal blessings in heaven. He promises to love you forever.

And because of His faithful character, He'll keep every single promise.

Reflecting on our missed reality TV opportunity, I can now see God's goodness in redirecting our path. He closed that door but opened many others. When He promises good for us, He means it! His promises are part of a larger intricate plan designed for our good and His glory.

When human promises crumble, God remains steady. He sees our hurt, understands our disappointments, and holds a beautiful future for us. He will always be faithful because it's His nature. It's who He is.

Trust the Promise Keeper.

— JUSTIN

A GRAVE CONCERN

Blessed be the God and Father of our Lord Jesus Christ! According to his great mercy, he has caused us to be born again to a living hope through the resurrection of Jesus Christ from the dead.

—1 PETER 1:3

I know you're just *dying* to read today's devotion. The topic is of *grave* importance. That's right—we're talking about our popular overnight coffin challenge!

For this video, Justin and I spent twenty-four hours in underground coffins. Justin got a $10,000 model. His "coffin" was a custom-built underground living space the size of a bedroom, complete with a TV, sofa, and mini fridge. As for me? Well, I got an actual coffin—a small wooden box worth $100.

Rats.

At the start, I thought, *Gosh, this isn't going to be too bad.* Thanks to LED lights inside, I wasn't in pitch darkness. And the crew provided various snacks and activities throughout.

But I was dead wrong.

While Justin was kickin' the bucket in style, I could barely move. It was hot during the day and cold at night. At one point, the crew gave Justin and me some "coffin companions." Justin got my dogs. I got a handful of live crickets. Seriously, guys?!

We tried to make twenty-four hours in a coffin as interesting and funny as possible. But the truth is, death is a serious matter. It's a consequence of our sin against God, and no one can escape it. Even in the funniest YouTube coffin challenges, the grave is never going to be a place where you want to stay permanently. Justin was just as ready to get out of his luxury coffin after the twenty-four hours was over.

Here's the good news: for followers of Jesus, death isn't a permanent destination. Through His death and resurrection, Jesus conquered death. He is forever alive in heaven, and Christians get to join Him there after life on earth. We get to keep on living with Him. And until it's your time to hang in heaven, Jesus is getting a special place ready so it's *perfect* for you.

Jesus' resurrection gives every Christian hope for the future and assurance of eternity in heaven. Death is not the end; it's just a pathway to an eternity beyond our wildest imaginations.

God offers this amazing-beyond-words future to you as a free gift through Jesus. Don't be caught coffin—er, coughin'—up this opportunity. Receive it in faith!

—ANDREW

A GUARANTEED WIN

> **But thanks be to God, who gives us the victory through our Lord Jesus Christ.**
> —1 CORINTHIANS 15:57

Here at JStu, we are all about games. From a massive game of hide-and-seek around our entire state of Colorado to playing capture the flag in the mountains, we've done it all. And in our spare time, we also play plenty of sports for fun like basketball and pickleball.

I love the rush of competing. But of course, it's even more fun when you win! The thrill of victory makes all the effort, danger, and sweat worth it. I've been fortunate to win a lot of the big team games we've done, including capture the flag. And thank goodness because losing is *really* annoying! (Sorry, Justin!)

Can you imagine what it would be like if you knew you had a guaranteed victory for a game you were about to play? What a relief from the pressure! If I knew I was going to win, I wouldn't worry about someone sprinting through the woods to grab my flag. I could just stand there with a big ol' smile on my face, rip off the other team's flag with ease, and send them all to jail. Ha!

It's one thing to be unsure of victory in games you play with your friends. It's an entirely different thing to be unsure of victory in life. If this life on earth were all there was, no big deal. But the

Bible says God created us with souls that exist for eternity. That's a *wee* bit longer than a statewide game of capture the flag, and it raises the stakes significantly!

Is this a game you're sure you're going to win? Thankfully, there's a way to be certain. As 1 Corinthians 15:57 says, God gives us victory through Jesus! That's not just a small win here or there. That's victory over the trials of life. That's victory over our greatest enemies—sin, Satan, and death! That's victory in both this life and the one to come.

This incredible victory can be yours when you believe in Jesus. He defeated all these enemies with His sacrificial death and amazing resurrection. And as our great Champion, He gives this same victory to everyone who asks Him to come into their lives.

Eternal victory means living confidently in the knowledge, faith, and joy that this forever-win is in the books—literally (Revelation 20:12).

Want to have a guaranteed victory in this life and the next? Play for Team Jesus!

— ANDREW

IS LIFE A GAME YOU'RE SURE YOU'RE GOING TO WIN?

WHAT COMES NEXT?

Remember the former things of old; for I am God, and there is no other; I am God, and there is none like me, declaring the end from the beginning and from ancient times things not yet done, saying, "My counsel shall stand, and I will accomplish all my purpose."
—ISAIAH 46:9–10

"Go forth to meet the shadowy future without fear and with a manly heart."

Those words come from famous nineteenth-century American poet Henry Wadsworth Longfellow. Or maybe SpongeBob, I can't remember. Either way, it's a great quote about the mysterious nature of the future.

We've all experienced both dread and anticipation of what the future might bring. One standout memory is when my wife, Brittany, gave birth to our first bundle of joy. Talk about nerves! Suddenly, a pressure cooker of emotions and uncertainties bubbled inside me. My mind overflowed with all the questions and responsibilities of being a rookie parent.

How do I raise this tiny human?

What if the baby does something we're not ready for?

Do babies come with instruction manuals?

How do I decode my daughter's cries?

And, *Good heavens, what's that awful smell?*

These were just a few of the questions that kept me up at night. Whether it's bracing for the whirlwind of a new baby, studying for that big math exam, or anticipating the championship game, jitters about the future are a regular part of life. But they don't have to be! We can find comfort in the fact that God holds our future with perfect wisdom and love.

Just as I (somehow!) survived the new-baby phase, God has been my anchor through all my swirling doubts—even when I didn't notice Him at the time. In my moments of feeling utterly incapable, God's strength has showed up.

God is in charge of the future. So the pressure is off me and you! That's a reality that brings me immense comfort. Because let's be honest, I'm not exactly the poster child for superhero strength. I stumble . . . a lot. But God never falters. His ways are righteous, and His plans are flawless.

But we need to be careful here. The fact that God knows the future doesn't mean we should simply lounge around and coast through life, hoping for the best without lifting a finger. No! God calls us to get to work and make good choices that honor Him. Somehow, He weaves our daily decisions into His master plan. Mind blown.

The future might be unclear to you. But that's okay! God has it under control. So trust Him for all your tomorrows. He will never let you down.

— JUSTIN

PACK SUNGLASSES

> For I know the plans I have for you, declares the LORD, plans for welfare and not for evil, to give you a future and a hope.
> —JEREMIAH 29:11

When we started making YouTube videos, Justin and I didn't really have a plan. We were just making videos for fun and laughs. But God had a plan for our channel all along.

JStu has grown so much. What started out as two goofballs running around with a camera has become a recognized business that supports multiple families—and now includes even more goofballs! It's amazing to look back on how God has blessed us.

And we're planning to expand. Even as we write this book, we're planning to build a new JStu warehouse. With a growing team and an ever-increasing stockpile of materials needed to make fun videos, we've outgrown our current office space. Hopefully more space will allow us to film more great videos for years to come.

Plans in life are important. Imagine going on a vacation with no preparation beforehand of where you're going. What if you packed for the beaches of Florida but ended up in the mountains of Colorado? The trip would be a disaster.

Plans are critical to navigate life. But life, as we all know,

ONLY GOD CAN MAKE *ANYTHING* HAPPEN.

doesn't always go according to plan. Thankfully, Scripture promises us that God has a good plan for our lives.

We can plan and try to strategize every last detail for the future, but ultimately, only God can make anything happen today, tomorrow, and in the years to come. This is good news! It means your life is in the hands of an all-powerful, all-knowing Creator. He loves you, and His plans for you can't be improved upon.

God doesn't wing it. His plans are perfectly ordered, beautifully detailed, and always for your ultimate good (Romans 8:28). His plans are to give you a good future filled with hope, peace, and countless other blessings. Through His Son, Jesus, you can have all of this—into eternity!

So go ahead and make plans for today, the rest of this week, and into the future that are honoring to God and true to the person He created you to be. But as you pursue these plans, remember that only God sees the future. And as you follow Him, no matter how your path might change, the future will look bright!

—ANDREW

WIRED FOR ETERNITY

God has made everything beautiful for its own time. He has planted eternity in the human heart, but even so, people cannot see the whole scope of God's work from beginning to end.

—ECCLESIASTES 3:11 NLT

Everybody wants a sweet ride.

Whether your taste is Lamborghini or Lexus, Jeep or Jaguar, Fiat or F-150, having a custom-made set of wheels is a ton of fun. So we took that idea and ran with it in classic JStu style.

Several years back, we purchased a toy car designed for kids and turned it into the ultimate ride for adults. We decked out this small-but-mighty beast on wheels with a killer sound system, glow lights underneath, and a fresh paint job. We took it everywhere—to a high school, a college campus, a fast-food drive-thru, a car dealership, and more. I can only imagine the envy in people's hearts as they watched us roll by—even if the max speed topped out at a couple miles per hour and our knees dangled awkwardly above the windshield.

One of the most painstaking jobs in preparing that car was wiring the high-end sound system, complete with a bumpin' sub-woofer. For the music to blast, the wires had to be meticulously and strategically placed throughout the car. No wiring, no sweet tunes.

Fresh mini cars aren't the only things that are intricately wired. God intentionally wired each of us with a longing to understand the future and what comes after this life. Before we were even born, He "installed" specific desires and curiosities in us, intending for them to draw us closer to Him.

Have you ever wondered what you'll be like in ten years? Or what job you'll have one day? Or who you'll marry? Or what happens after death? Or what heaven will be like? We all have! And these aren't random thoughts. God has wired your brain for the future—and for eternity.

Your life isn't a product of chance, and your future isn't a guessing game. God has a plan for you. He desires a relationship with you through His Son, Jesus, and He wants you to spend eternity with Him in heaven. To lovingly move you in that direction, He has put questions, curiosities, and longings in your heart.

Isn't that amazing? Out of His great love, God has wired us with desires for more than we know here on earth—desires that only He can satisfy. So keep pondering the future as you seek Him through prayer and Scripture. Your future is in His hands, and in Jesus, it's an awfully good one!

— JUSTIN

THE GREATEST 1-UP

> He will swallow up death forever; and the Lord God will wipe away tears from all faces, and the reproach of his people he will take away from all the earth.
> —ISAIAH 25:8

Everyone has fears in life. When you were little, you were probably scared of the dark. Some people can't do heights. Other people start to sweat at the thought of small spaces. Some people have an arresting fear of clowns. And trust me, there *is* something slightly disturbing about painted faces and giant shoes.

Then, of course, there's arachnophobia—the fear of spiders. They're legit creepy! So for one of our early YouTube videos, Justin and I took that idea and ran with it. We'd sneak up on people at a local college campus and scare them with fake spiders. Lots of them jumped and screamed. And more than a few used some potty language. Overall, the reactions were hilarious.

We often fear what we don't know, what we can't control, or what we think could be harmful. But even if spiders don't make you gasp, every human has a lingering concern about—or downright fear of—death.

But if you have put your faith in Jesus, you don't have to be afraid! Look at Isaiah 25:8. This is an amazing Old Testament promise of what Jesus would accomplish when He came to earth. By living a perfect life, dying on the cross, and rising three days later, Jesus conquered death itself! And because Jesus lives forever, He promises the same eternal life to each person who puts their faith in Him. It's the greatest 1-up you'll ever discover!

Of course, everyone still physically dies. Our lives on earth will end one day, and our bodies will be buried and fade away. But the Bible says our souls—the invisible spirits inside us—will live forever. And one day, He'll return to bring all His followers to heaven, where He'll be with us forever and give us heavenly bodies that will never weaken or die. Amazing!

Having no fear in death is easier said than done. But when we realize what awaits us as believers, it begins to take away death's terror. Because of Jesus' resurrection, death looks more like a harmless fake spider than a huge black widow getting ready to strike.

So trust in God's promise of everlasting life in Jesus. Thanks to the Savior, we don't have anything to fear in this life or the one to come!

— ANDREW

YOU DON'T HAVE TO BE AFRAID OF DEATH.

BETTER THAN EVERYTHING

"For behold, I create new heavens and a
new earth, and the former things shall not
be remembered or come into mind."
—ISAIAH 65:17

Have you ever had a jaw-dropping moment that left you in awe?
For me, it was our trip to Iceland for an incredible video shoot
at the Thridrangar Lighthouse. Our journey to this wild location
was a hair-raising experience. Initially, I was a bundle of nerves,
but as the journey unfolded, the fear faded, and I found myself
immersed in a breathtaking landscape.

The helicopter flight alone was well worth the price of admis-
sion. But once we got to the lighthouse, I was overwhelmed by
the majestic beauty all around me—warm sun, crystal-clear skies,
serene isolation, and even a sea lion gracefully swimming in the
surf below. It was an absolute *wow* moment!

Yet in all the grandeur, one thing was missing: the joy of sharing it with my wife and kids. Because we all want to experience
those mountaintop—or isolated European lighthouse—moments
with those we love.

That's why I can't wait for heaven! For every believer, God
promises a beyond-description experience in His presence forever. That beats lighthouses, helicopter rides, and sea lions any day!

Heaven isn't just a concept or a fairy-tale ending; it's a guaranteed future for us Christians. And it will be beyond our wildest imaginations, a place filled with boundless blessings and joy. Think about it: no more sickness, tears, pain, or loss—just endless goodness, beauty, and fun. Sounds like a place you'd never want to leave, right? And the best part is, we'll get to see God face-to-face and soak in His glory forever.

Some people mistakenly think heaven will eventually get boring since it will last for, you know, all eternity. But that's not the case at all! Being in the actual presence of God the Father, Son, and Holy Spirit is something that will never grow old. Take your best day ever, multiply that joy by infinity, and that's a small glimpse of what awaits every follower of Jesus in the life to come!

Not even the most splendid of earthly moments—including breathtaking Icelandic lighthouses—can compare to what awaits us in the eternity that God has promised. So let those awe-inspiring moments in this life be a glimpse—a trailer, if you will—of the eternal joy that lies ahead. Your earthly journey might be short and temporary, but the eternal destination is beyond imagination!

—JUSTIN

CREATE A TIME CAPSULE

This challenge is all about time. But it's less TikTok and more *tick-tock ticktock*. So now it's time (*heh, heh*) to make history!

A time capsule is a container of items that show the person who finds the container in the future (perhaps you!) what life is like today. If you want someone else to find your capsule, bury it in your yard or hide it somewhere it won't be found for at least a few years. If your capsule is for future *you*—as a way to remember who you were and what you were like at this age—tuck it away in your closet, basement, or garage.

DIRECTIONS

1. Find a container with a lid. It can be as simple as a shoebox, but if you're going to bury it outside, make sure it seals tightly and won't decompose.
2. Mark your name and the date on the outside of the capsule.
3. Fill it up!

CONTENT IDEAS

- a photo of you and/or your family
- a photo of your pets
- a favorite shirt you've outgrown
- a favorite childhood toy
- an ad or catalog for toys or clothing
- a favorite book, magazine, or comic
- a list of your favorite songs or movies
- a recent art project
- something that represents your favorite sport or hobby
- a souvenir from a concert or sporting event you attended
- an outdated piece of technology
- a Bible
- a copy of your favorite Bible verse
- a copy of a poem or story you've written
- coins
- a newspaper or copies of today's news stories
- a note describing what you think the future will be like
- a letter to your future self or a letter to the person who finds your capsule

A HARD FALL

> For we know that the whole creation has been
> groaning together in the pains of childbirth
> until now. And not only the creation, but we
> ourselves, who have the firstfruits of the Spirit,
> groan inwardly as we wait eagerly for adoption
> as sons, the redemption of our bodies.
> **—ROMANS 8:22–23**

Physical comedy—everything from wiping out on a bike to falling completely on your face out of nowhere—is always good for some chuckles. So early on in our JStu career, we did a series of falling videos. We'd approach unsuspecting customers at a grocery store, often carrying a teetering tower of items, and perform some ridiculously exaggerated falls. It was hilarious! Shoppers were usually stunned speechless, or they'd ask, "Are you okay?" One lady told us, "Don't worry, hon. I do that almost every day."

One particular fall stands out as my favorite. Armed with about twenty orange pumpkin pails during Halloween season, I sprinted down an aisle and tumbled, sending the trick-or-treat buckets flying everywhere. It was utter mayhem.

I've lost track of the countless falls we've done over the years. But it does make me wonder: *Is this why my bones constantly ache?*

We did those falls for laughs, but there's a fall that's much more serious. Genesis 3 describes the moment when Adam and Eve, the first humans, sinned against God by eating forbidden fruit. Ever since then, sin has corrupted every human heart—and the world itself. From backyard weeds to global wars, the trials and struggles of life are part of living in a sin-stained world.

Dealing with a trouble-filled world can feel overwhelming at times. Maybe you come from a difficult family situation. Maybe a loved one is struggling with a serious illness. Or some kids at school just won't stop bullying you. The trials of life are real and hard. Romans 8:22 acknowledges this when it says the very earth itself is "groaning" under the weight of sin.

It can be easy to blame God for the trials we experience. But while God allows difficult times in our lives to strengthen our faith, He's never responsible for bad human choices. He lets people make their own decisions, and often there are consequences that hurt others.

Here's the good news: one day, Jesus will come back to make all things new! When He does, He'll bring all His children into an eternal existence free of sin, pain, and death. No more family strife! No more sickness! No more bullies!

No more trials and suffering!

This broken world and its painful falls won't last forever. Trust in the coming Savior. Lean on Him. Cry out to Him. He is faithful. Jesus will return and when He does, all human suffering will stop—forever!

— JUSTIN

TOUGH TIMES, GOOD GOD

> I trust in you, O LORD; I say, "You are my God."
> —PSALM 31:14

Have you ever watched our impossible maze video? If not, buckle up for the challenge of a lifetime!

The challenge was simple: two teams, a $10,000 prize, and a maze that'd make your GPS cry. Twists, turns, dead ends, and a whole lot of laughs—it was an a-maze-ing masterpiece!

At times life feels like an impossible labyrinth with no escape route. Trials pop up without warning. Setbacks feel overwhelming. Dead ends are frustrating and exhausting.

But here's a truth bomb that'll echo through any twisting tunnel: trials are mysterious and maddening, but God is good. If that sounds a bit simplistic, read it again. No matter what happens in life, *God . . . is . . . good.*

This perspective is super important to remember when you're suffering. Knowing that God's character doesn't change can help you feel steady in the storm—*any* storm.

As you navigate difficulties, don't forget that God exists above the chaos. He knows all, sees all, and carves a path for us to take. Even when you feel like you can't keep going, you can count on God's goodness, love, and power.

So the next time you feel lost in life's maze, take a step back,

GOD EXISTS ABOVE THE CHAOS.

knowing that God is in the crazy with you and He'll never lead you down a wrong path. You can trust Him around every corner.

When the winners emerged from the JStu maze, the cash prize was pretty sweet. But Christians have a far greater reward waiting for them at the end of the maze of life—eternity with the Lord!

So keep pushing through. You're not done yet! Life might feel like a confusing network of paths that go nowhere. But with God as your guide, you'll make it. You've already won. You've got this, and the ultimate prize is just around the bend.

— JUSTIN

THE GOD WHO IS NEAR

**The Lord is near to all who call on him,
to all who call on him in truth.**
—PSALM 145:18

Most folks cringe at the thought of small spaces, and it's completely understandable. Yet for us at JStu, the idea of filming a video that pushes us out of our comfort zone is always an exciting challenge. So Andrew, Isaac, and I embarked on a wild journey: enduring one hundred hours in a survival bunker!

Of course, typical to our style, we didn't settle for just *any* bunker. We kept downgrading to smaller and smaller spaces until we found ourselves crammed into the tiniest box imaginable. The three of us barely fit inside, attempting to move was nearly impossible, and claustrophobia soon began kicking in. It was a challenge in every sense of the word, but the video was unforgettable.

This brings to mind the wonderful truth of Psalm 145:18: God is close to all who call on Him. This is incredible! God rules over the entire universe He created. Galaxies cannot contain Him. He is highly exalted over all He has made.

Yet He's not a distant God. He is near to everyone who asks for His presence. He draws near to us because He loves us and knows we're lost without Him. He anticipates all our troubles, and He's ready to guide us through them.

Unlike being close to other fully grown men in a survival bunker challenge for more than four days, being close to God isn't uncomfortable! It's quite the opposite. In the cramped bunker, I *definitely* wanted distance from my friends (no offense, guys). But God's nearness brings peace and joy and strengthens our faith.

You learn a lot about people in tight quarters! The same is true with God. When you're in a tight spot in life, remember that God is always close by. His power and love shine brightest in our moments of fear and doubt. He is offering you the ultimate comfort. So lean on Him and trust that He's got everything under control. Finding rest in God's nearness is a beautifully small, safe place you'll never want to leave.

— JUSTIN

GOD'S POWER AND LOVE SHINE BRIGHTEST IN OUR MOMENTS OF FEAR AND DOUBT.

NO PAIN, NO GAIN

Count it all joy, my brothers, when you meet trials
of various kinds, for you know that the testing
of your faith produces steadfastness. And let
steadfastness have its full effect, that you may
be perfect and complete, lacking in nothing.
—JAMES 1:2–4

The Hunger Games is a pretty awesome book and movie series. But imagine playing *The Hunger Games* in real life! How cool would that be? (You know, minus the actual deaths.)

That's what we thought too!

In the winter of 2024, we traveled to a remote patch of untamed wilderness in Colorado with twenty-one people, all competing to be the last person standing in the ultimate battle. To do so, we had to run around a hundred acres of snowy, wooded landscape and find foam weapons to eliminate each other. It was amazing!

The entire contest took about twenty hours, and it was intense! One competitor was eliminated within seconds. Swords were swinging and arrows were flying everywhere. I made an early alliance with my brother and a friend, which paid off big-time. For one day, I felt like a real-life gladiator! And if you want to know who won, well, watch the video!

It's easy to be joyful when we're out making videos like that. But life isn't always playing super-fun outdoor games with your friends. Like the fictional contestants of *The Hunger Games* experienced, life can sometimes feel like there's trouble around every turn.

Yet God tells us to "count it all joy . . . when you meet trials of various kinds" (James 1:2). What? Is God telling you that you're supposed to be happy when you get sick or your best friend ditches you or a close family member dies? No. God knows trials are hard, and He doesn't expect you to love the pain. He's telling you to look at the bigger picture.

God allows trials in our lives to build our faith. Trials produce *steadfastness*, which means being firm or loyal in your belief. As you look to God in your trials, you'll develop patience, perseverance, trust in Him, and many other godly characteristics. You'll become stronger in your faith. This is why we can "count it all joy" when trouble comes!

Like a swift foam sword to the head when you aren't looking, trials often come when you least expect them. But as you trust in God, you can make it through every single one. When your faith is tested, you'll be standing strong in the end, joyfully seeing how God gave you steadfastness every step of the way.

— ANDREW

STRENGTH IN WEAKNESS

He said to me, "My grace is sufficient for you, for my power is made perfect in weakness." Therefore I will boast all the more gladly of my weaknesses, so that the power of Christ may rest upon me. For the sake of Christ, then, I am content with weaknesses, insults, hardships, persecutions, and calamities. For when I am weak, then I am strong.

—2 CORINTHIANS 12:9-10

Have you ever wanted to hike up a mountain? Me either. But we did it anyway.

Near where we live, there's an ascent nicknamed "the Incline." I think a more fitting name would be "the Staircase of Doom." This trek has more than 2,500 stairsteps that stretch out for nearly a mile, and many people have been injured on this hike.

After about two hours of walking, we barely made it to the top. We were out of breath, our legs felt like jelly, and we were completely exhausted. The exhilaration of the accomplishment was quickly replaced by this harrowing thought: *Now we've got to go back the way we came.* At this point, I felt like a football coach was yelling at me, *You thought* climbing *was tough?* In that moment, I felt pretty weak.

We often look at weakness as a bad thing. Who wants to be

weak at the gym, on the ball field, or in gaming? But what if I told you God sees our weakness differently?

You see, God's power truly goes on display in our weakest moments.

That sounds like a contradiction—an absurdity that simply *can't* be true. But it is! God's amazing love, power, and grace shine brightest against the backdrop of our limitations. When we're powerless, God is powerful. Where our understanding ends, His wisdom is limitless. When we don't think we can take another step up (or down!) the mountain, He gives us strength for the journey.

You will experience many times of weakness in life. The question is, what will you do in those moments? Will you attempt to push forward in your own power? (Spoiler alert: not a great idea!) Or will you seek the Lord?

God is a genius, a stacked tough guy, and a superhero all in one. Why would we try to do things on our own when we have His unlimited power and wisdom at our disposal? Whether you feel weak or strong, put away your pride and ask God Almighty to do the work.

Don't attempt to climb the mountains of life in your own strength, or you'll surely fall down. Trust in His strength. When you do, the mountain peak doesn't seem as ominous. Keep climbing and clinging to Jesus to get to the top!

— JUSTIN

PUTTING FEAR IN ITS PLACE

Fear not, for I am with you; be not dismayed, for I am your God; I will strengthen you, I will help you, I will uphold you with my righteous right hand.
—ISAIAH 41:10

I don't know about you, but I'd rather not get eaten by a shark. For one of our videos, that terrifying thought actually became a possibility!

In 2022, my buddy Caleb and I traveled to a remote island off the coast of Florida without food, water, or any basic survival gear. Our challenge? To get off the island by building a raft using the only supply we brought: duct tape. The nearest inhabited land was a mile away. On the boat ride to the island, our driver told us this particular area was a popular feeding ground for sharks. *Gulp.*

Using driftwood and other junk that had washed ashore, Caleb and I constructed perhaps the most unseaworthy vessel in the history of maritime travel. It was only big enough for one person, so I set sail alone, hoping to flag down a boat to go back for Caleb—assuming I survived the adventure myself.

After making it past the main breaker waves, my raft tipped over. Bobbing up and down in the water, I started thinking about my worst fear—those dorsal-finned predators of the deep. Panic set in. And then—well, watch the video to find out what happened!

Floating in the ocean after my raft had capsized was one of the most terrifying moments in my life. Fear is a normal and often helpful human emotion, especially when we're in potentially dangerous situations. But often our fears, worries, and anxieties are unwarranted and keep us from doing good things or moving forward in life.

In Isaiah 41:10, God tells us not to fear because He is with us. He is bigger than any fear we might have, and His promise to strengthen and help us can bring us relief and peace when we're stressed or anxious.

When we let fear take over our minds, what we're really saying is, *God, I know You can do a lot. But I'm not sure You can handle this problem.* And of course, that's not true. There is no difficulty bigger than He is; there's nothing He can't handle.

Now, that doesn't mean we should do anything reckless, expecting Him to save us from our foolishness. Don't take a dip in chum-filled waters with hungry sharks! But it does mean that God will help us overcome our fears. Jesus conquered our greatest enemies (sin, Satan, and death), so clearly He can help you overcome anything.

No matter what challenge you're facing at home, at school, or anywhere (even a deserted island!), trust in God. He will most certainly uphold you with His righteous right hand.

—ANDREW

REFUGE IN THE STORM

> Be merciful to me, O God, be merciful to me, for in you my soul takes refuge; in the shadow of your wings I will take refuge, till the storms of destruction pass by.
> —PSALM 57:1

Since we've made hundreds of YouTube videos over the years, you might think I'd have a tough time picking my favorite—let alone remembering them all!

Nope.

My favorite video is an easy choice because it's perhaps the scariest one we've ever done! Imagine spending the night in an old, crumbling hotel. Then add the fact that this "hotel" is actually a rickety, rusty oil rig in the middle of the ocean, thirty-five miles from shore. It was scary epicness on a whole new level!

To ratchet up the intensity, we visited this cozy little house of horrors when high winds were creating big, rolling waves. With every gust of wind, the rig's rusted metal creaked and swayed. It was a rollicking adventure on the high seas!

But I was terrified. As we set up for the night ahead, my mind couldn't help but think about all the *what-ifs*.

What if the hotel does a cannonball into the ocean?

What if we end up being real-life castaways?

What if the kraken is real—and attacks us?

Okay, I didn't really think that last one. But the dangers and unknowns were real!

In the midst of it all, Psalm 57:1 came to the rescue. This verse is a beautiful, calming reminder. It's like God is telling us, *It's all right. I got this*. In the midst of my fears, I found refuge in God's Word.

Life, with all its trials and problems, can be like sailing on a dinghy in storm-tossed waters. But God's Word and His promises are our life preserver. Scripture is packed with powerful truths and much-needed reminders for when life goes all hurricane mode and the waves look like they're auditioning for a blockbuster disaster movie.

When those fears and *what-ifs* start swimming around in your head, redirect your focus to the One who can help by diving into His Word. You're not facing storms alone. You're navigating them with a God who's the ultimate refuge. He's the Lord God Almighty, Maker of heaven and earth, Calmer of waves and Silencer of storms.

— JUSTIN

HERE ARE A FEW OTHER VERSES TO BUILD YOUR COURAGE:
- PSALM 46:1–3
- PHILIPPIANS 4:6–7
- JAMES 1:2–4

HAND IT OVER

Cast all your anxiety on him because he cares for you.

—1 PETER 5:7 NIV

The year 2020 was pretty weird. That's when the COVID-19 pandemic shut down the world.

Early on, there was a lot of uncertainty and questions. *How can I avoid getting COVID? What happens if I do get it? Will I die? Will my family members die? How can I stop the spread of the virus? When will it end?*

Stores, offices, churches, and other public places shut their doors. You couldn't go anywhere without a mask, and no one knew if it was going to get worse. Lots of questions, not many answers.

I had a moment when I struggled with the isolation we were all experiencing. My family wasn't getting together. My friends weren't hanging out. And we had to stop making videos for a while. I felt anxious, alone, and scared.

But I remembered that the Bible tells us to cast our cares on God. So I prayed about my COVID-related anxieties. It wasn't a general *Be with us today* kind of prayer. Instead, I asked specifically that He would watch over me, my family, and my friends. I asked Him to walk with us during the pandemic.

As soon as I finished praying, God reminded me of another verse—one I hadn't read in years. It was Isaiah 43:2: "When you

> ## GOD CAN HANDLE WHATEVER YOU BRING TO HIM.

pass through the waters, I will be with you." I immediately felt His peace and His care for me.

The pandemic eventually subsided, my family made it through okay, and life returned to normal. We went back to the grocery store, started attending church services again, and scheduled time to get together with family and friends. Oh, and JStu filming resumed!

Whether your cares and anxieties stem from a global pandemic or something more personal, cast them all on God. He cares about you. He wants you to bring your concerns to Him in prayer.

God is all-powerful and perfectly wise. He can handle whatever you bring to Him. You are His child and He loves you, so it's not a burden for Him to take your worries and concerns. He's ready to answer your prayers and give you peace.

—ANDREW

FOR THE GOOD

And we know that for those who love God
all things work together for good, for those
who are called according to his purpose.
—ROMANS 8:28

Let me share with you the story of how I became a YouTuber.

Years ago, I was working in a program for children of service personnel at an Air Force base in Colorado while also attending film school. I enjoyed my job and loved working with kids, but I was also doing YouTube videos with Justin in my spare time.

My dad, brother, and I were planning to visit my grandma in Ohio on an upcoming weekend. While there, we wanted to catch an Ohio State football game and an NFL game—the Cincinnati Bengals versus my beloved Denver Broncos! I asked for time off weeks in advance and made preparations. It was going to be one of the best weekends ever!

But a couple days before my trip, my boss told me that I couldn't take those days off for my trip. I was so mad and disappointed. I missed out on visiting my grandma and enjoying a fun weekend of football. I've still never been to an Ohio State football game.

Reeling from the disappointment, I began evaluating what I wanted to do in life. I quit my job and started pursuing YouTube.

God has done some incredible things with our channel, and I'm glad I made the switch. Looking back, that frustrating experience was the launching point for a career that I love.

Life is full of painful experiences. That's just how it is. You've probably been through hard times already, and sadly, there will be more to come. In the moment, we often wonder why God allows these challenging moments in our lives.

But remember this: God works out all things for the good of those who love Him. Not just some things. Or a couple things here and there. Or even the majority of things. He works *all things* for our good!

How does God do this? Well, I'm not actually sure. A trial might last for days, weeks, months—or even longer. And you might never fully understand God's designs. After all, He's God and we're not! But God is going to achieve His purpose every time, and it's always—always!—for your good. That's pretty incredible.

In the moment, that canceled trip hurt badly. But look what God did in my life! He's going to do good for you in His own way and in His own time. Today might be hard. But trust Him. One day, you'll see how God worked in your life—all for your good!

— ANDREW

THE END OF TROUBLES

"He will wipe away every tear from their eyes, and death shall be no more, neither shall there be mourning, nor crying, nor pain anymore, for the former things have passed away."
—REVELATION 21:4

There's sometimes a hidden side to our videos that we don't showcase. Behind the scenes, accidental injuries and moments of pain happen that never make it through edits. One particularly memorable incident for me was when I got stapled in the arm.

We were using staple guns to tack up something during a shoot. Caught up in the moment, I playfully pretended to staple others with an empty stapler. Probably not my best idea ever. A few moments later, one of my friends reciprocated, unaware that his staple gun was loaded. Public safety announcement: being stapled in the arm really hurts!

Pain and suffering are familiar companions in life. Often, the hurt we experience comes from others' poor choices, making the sting feel even worse. But we all also go through sickness, death, accidents, and our own bad decisions. Life is hard!

Yet I find great comfort in knowing that my pain is only temporary. When Jesus returns, He will destroy all evil, renew His creation, and welcome all His followers into a new heaven and new earth. We'll live there forever in the presence of God Himself. This new home will be free of all sin, sadness, pain, suffering, disease, death—and yeah, I imagine there won't be any staple gun mishaps there either. (Although I like to think there will be funny pranks!)

The promise of a perfect forever with God fills my mind with hope. Despite the continued presence of pain in this world, we can trust that our future existence will be far different. Pain and suffering will be a distant memory. This reality offers peace and strength for the challenges we face today.

As you endure pain and suffering, keep trusting the Lord. Keep your eye on that glorious future, what the apostle Paul calls "the heavenly prize" (Philippians 3:14 NLT). And remember that the sufferings of this life can't even compare to the glories of the life to come (Romans 8:18). As you keep this heavenly hope fresh in your mind, you'll be encouraged, you'll build spiritual endurance, and your faith will grow.

Thanks to Jesus, the future for all believers is a dream to look forward to—and it's free of staple gun surprises!

— **JUSTIN**

OUTDOOR OVERNIGHT SURVIVAL CHALLENGE

What scares you? Perhaps it's the dark, the unknown, creepy-crawly critters, or going without Wi-Fi. Well, it's time to face your fears—and do something super-fun—with an extreme backpacking challenge! Your mission: backpack to a campsite somewhere in the wilderness (the deeper, darker, and scarier, the better!) and survive the night.

GET PREPARED

1. Find a trusted adult to take you backpacking, and get permission from your grown-up.
2. Choose a trail. Make sure you can carry all your gear the distance of the trail to the backpacking campsite.
3. Pack your gear.
4. Go forth and conquer!

SUPPLIES

Your supplies will depend on the weather forecast, where you're going, and what you'll be doing. Here are the essentials:

- backpack (that's a no-brainer!)
- comfortable, sturdy walking shoes
- map of the trail and your campsite
- drinking water
- first aid kit
- tent
- sleeping bag
- sleeping pad or yoga mat
- pillow
- flashlight
- lantern
- extra batteries
- drinking water
- (enough for your whole trip or bring a water filter pump)
- change of clothes
- jacket
- meals
- *must . . . have . . . snacks!*

CAMPFIRE COOKING

If campfires are allowed at your site, bring supplies and help an adult build a fire. Then dine in style.

- Roast hot dogs or kebabs.
- Make s'mores.
- Heat water and make hot chocolate.
- Make foil pack breakfast burritos.

ACTIVITIES

Being outdoors at night can be a little spooky! Tackle your fears and have some fun doing it with any of these options:

- Play hide-and-seek.
- Play ghost in the graveyard.
- Tell spooky stories.
- Use a smartphone to film a scary movie!
- Go on a hike in the dark.

Next level: Go for the weekend (or longer!) instead of just one night.

HONOR CODE

> Children, obey your parents in the Lord, for this is
> right. "Honor your father and mother" (this is the
> first commandment with a promise), "that it may go
> well with you and that you may live long in the land."
> —EPHESIANS 6:1–3

Have you ever tried to make pancakes, build a desk, or (*gulp*) drive while not being able to see, hear, or talk? Well, leave to it JStu to try them all!

For one of our videos, Andrew, Isaac, and yours truly attempted these tasks together, but with a twist—Andrew wore sightless goggles, Isaac wore noise-canceling headphones, and I got slapped with a big piece of duct tape over my mouth. We had to somehow work together to accomplish those tasks while each of us was limited in a sense or means of communication.

Let's just say it was more "epic fail" than "mission accomplished"! Every task seemed super hard. Every interaction became a challenge. Communication felt impossible. We couldn't understand each other at all!

Have you ever felt like a parent, teacher, or someone else ignored everything you said or did? Have you ever thought, *They just don't understand me. It's so hard to connect with them. So why even bother?*

We've all been there.

And while no adult in your life is perfect, God's design for the world gives adults authority over kids. God's command to honor and obey our parents is really basic training for submitting to His authority in our lives. If we can't obey those we *can* see (like our parents), how can we obey the God we *can't* see? When we blindfold ourselves to their wisdom, close our ears to their advice, or forget how to talk respectfully, we're essentially setting ourselves up for challenge-level struggles.

God calls us to something better. Obeying authority is like a cheat code for easier navigation in life! It's about us becoming more like Jesus, the Son of God, who also submitted to God the Father in all things.

Just like in our "Can't See, Can't Hear, Can't Talk" video, you're not always going to connect or communicate perfectly with your parents, teachers, and other authority figures. They're going to make decisions that aren't perfect because *they're* not perfect! Still, your job is to honor and obey them with humility and respect. As you do this, you'll learn to honor and obey God, which is the ultimate goal!

—JUSTIN

SOMETIMES *HONORING* ISN'T THE SAME AS *OBEYING*. IF YOUR PARENT OR OTHER ADULT TELLS YOU TO DO SOMETHING YOU KNOW IS WRONG, TALK TO AN ADULT YOU TRUST TO GET HELP.

GOOD SURROUNDINGS

A friend loves at all times, and a brother is born for adversity.
—PROVERBS 17:17

Justin and I have been friends for nearly twenty years. I'm very thankful that God has brought us close together. This is true in the literal sense too—we're next-door neighbors! We've been able to keep a strong friendship for two decades because we both try to love at all times and be there for each other in times of adversity. There's nothing like a good friend.

Having friends who love God is *so* important for your faith. God didn't create us to live alone like hermits in the mountains with no interactions with others. He created us to have community, enjoying all the laughs, joys, companionship, spiritual growth, and memories that strong friendships can bring.

You can't choose everything in life, but you can choose your friends! So make good choices. Other than your family, there is perhaps no greater influence on your life than the friends you choose.

True friends ride by your side during all the hardships that life brings. A good friend makes you better (Proverbs 27:17). A good friend will love you through fun times and hard times. A good friend will be quick to forgive when you screw up. A good friend

A GOOD FRIEND MAKES YOU BETTER.

will help you grow closer to God. Even as I was writing this, our friend Seth ("Hyper") texted me to ask what he can pray about for me.

Are these the qualities you see in the people you surround yourself with? If the people you run with disrespect authority, gossip, show unkindness to others, disappear when you're struggling, and lead you away from God, you'll need to make some changes in your circle. Finding friends who encourage and strengthen you might take some time, but that's okay. It's so worth it.

To have good friends, you must be one yourself! Be a friend who loves at all times and is born for adversity. Sharpen others in their walk with the Lord as you seek to do the same in your life. As you do this and surround yourself with others who love Jesus too, you can enjoy wonderful friendships that last a lifetime!

—ANDREW

THE GOLDEN RULE

"Whatever you wish that others would do to you, do also to them."
—MATTHEW 7:12

In our early years of JStu, we did plenty of public pranks. Lots of them were hilarious, but some of our ideas were probably borderline too much. For example, we did a video where we pretended to trip or sneeze, and then spilled popcorn all over people. The reactions we got were pretty funny, and most people were gracious in their responses. Some people even helped us clean up the popcorn and put it back in our bowls! But we also made a lot of greasy messes.

While the video was good for some chuckles, perhaps it wasn't the best example of the Golden Rule. Found in Matthew 7:12, the famous Golden Rule tells us, quite simply, to treat others the way we want to be treated.

How believers interact with people is really important. The Golden Rule is a simple, uncomplicated way of living out what Jesus called "the second greatest commandment"—love others as you love yourself (Matthew 22:39). Of course, it's not always easy because our sinful pride, selfishness, and anger often get in the way.

Before doing or saying something, it's always a good habit

to ask yourself, *Would I like it if someone did or said that to me?* This is true in the online world as much as it is in person. We have received endless amounts of hate comments on our videos, and I always wonder if the sender would appreciate a similar comment directed at them. Probably not.

It's easy to be rude and mean-spirited online or through a text. Somehow we think that there aren't any consequences because the person isn't physically present. But a real person, with real feelings and emotions, still reads what you write. The Golden Rule applies across all forms of communication!

Galatians 6:7 says we reap what we sow. In other words, you get what you plant. What you throw out at people will boomerang back to you. If you dish out unkindness, sarcasm, put-downs, mean-spirited jokes, and anger, you'll likely get that in return. That's also why it's so much better to dish out love, kindness, and encouragement! The Golden Rule benefits you as well as others.

So don't send your popcorn—or unkindness—flying at others. Treat people with love and respect, just as you want them to treat you.

—ANDREW

169

CREATED EQUAL

The LORD sees not as man sees: man looks on the outward appearance, but the LORD looks on the heart.
—1 SAMUEL 16:7

At JStu, we love survival challenges. It's always a blast to get creative with crazy limitations and go up against the elements. In one particularly wacky survival challenge, Isaac and I tried surviving twenty-four hours in the dead of winter with gear in just one color.

We had to buy all our survival items—food, clothing, shelter, everything!—in our assigned color. Isaac got red, one of the most universal colors in the world. And me? I got purple.

I know, I know—stop laughing.

Could there be a *worse* choice for survival gear and food than purple? I mean, really—how was I supposed to find anything good in that color? In the end, I managed to find some, uh, interesting purple items, and we enjoyed a hilarious experience.

Trying to survive outdoors with only purple gear on a night when temperatures dipped into the low twenties was like playing life on hard mode! It would've been so much better with more colors.

The same is true in life. God didn't make a one-color world. He created a world of beautiful diversity, filled with people who look different and have different experiences, all gloriously made in His image.

God isn't into the outer appearance game; He's all about our hearts. In a world where people tend to judge others by the way they look or where they're from, it's important to remember that God's love doesn't play favorites. Every human on earth is beautiful because they are made in His image. Each person is precious and valuable because God declares it so.

In heaven, people of every nation, background, wealth bracket, education level, and skin tone worship at God's throne (Revelation 7:9). That's what God's idea of perfection looks like. Here on earth, we can bring a bit of heaven down by valuing all types of people and building relationships with people who are different from us.

So love others with God's impartial love. Look at others as God sees them. Skip the surface-level judgments, and value each person as a fellow image-bearer of our Creator. Jesus died for people of all races, ethnicities, and backgrounds, just like He died for you.

Thankfully, we don't live in a one-color world. Praise God for that and seek to love others as He does!

— JUSTIN

GROUNDED

> "Everyone then who hears these words of mine and does them will be like a wise man who built his house on the rock. And the rain fell, and the floods came, and the winds blew and beat on that house, but it did not fall, because it had been founded on the rock."
>
> —MATTHEW 7:24-25

We love coming up with extreme scenarios for our videos. For one survival challenge, I picked the most outrageous location I could think of to spend the night alone: the middle of a frozen lake. The ice was super slippery, and the temperature was barely over 0 degrees.

I drug the first load of supplies out on the lake and started setting up my inflatable tent. The wind was blowing at warp speed, but I had come prepared. I pounded stakes into the ice to keep the tent in place. Except ... the wind ripped the stakes out and nearly blew my tent away! (Why did I bring a tent that was basically a balloon?) I even tried anchoring the tent to some nearby rocks. But the tent just slid around on the ice. So I gave up. I packed up my gear and moved to a spot off the lake and out of the wind. I realized that my tent was never going to stay still on that icy lake. The ice was a terrible foundation for a campsite.

When Jesus talked about foundations, He wasn't speaking of

actual houses or campsites. He was teaching people to base their lives on Him. One way to do that is to build your relationships on solid ground. That doesn't mean all of your friends need to be Christians, but it does mean that your relationships start from a place of respect, honesty, and kindness.

Have you ever tried to make friends with a popular kid by pretending to like something you don't actually like? That's a slippery foundation. You can't really be friends with someone who doesn't know and respect the real you.

Or maybe you've hung out with kids who play mean pranks or talk badly about other people. Those kids aren't acting like Jesus, and they might get you in trouble. That's a shaky place to be.

Instead, spend your energy building solid relationships based on Jesus' love and wisdom! Surround yourself with people who think you're awesome and help you be your best self. When life gets slippery, you'll be glad to have friends who help keep you grounded.

— ANDREW

24-HOUR ONE-ROOM CHALLENGE

In many JStu challenges, we spend a long time together in very small spaces—like so small we can smell each other's breath. *Ew.* But breath mints aside, we've gotten really close over all those hours together in close quarters.

Choose a friend and put your relationship building into overdrive by spending twenty-four hours in the same room!

GET PREPARED

1. Pick the room. This could be a basement, your bedroom, or another room in one of your homes. It doesn't have to be as small as a JStu microhotel, but we're not going for the Taj Mahal either! Something in the middle should do nicely.
2. Make a plan for food. Either pack food that will last the whole time, or ask a family member to bring meals to you.
3. Stock the room with some sweet snackage. Must . . . have . . . snacks!
4. Decide on everyone's sleeping space. Nobody wants a grumpy, sleep-deprived argument at one A.M. over who has to snooze on the floor!
5. Pack clothes, toiletries, medicines, and anything else you'll need.
6. Plan your activities and gather or buy any materials you'll need.

ACTIVITY IDEAS

- Build something cool—a LEGO set, a STEM kit, the world's biggest tower of random household items (no glass!).
- Play your favorite card and board games.
- Play two truths and a lie.
- Learn new games.
- Build the world's biggest pillow-and-blanket fort.
- Pick a classic fairy tale, such as *Goldilocks and*

ⓘ Bathroom breaks are allowed and are also highly encouraged.

the *Three Bears*, *Little Red Riding Hood*, or *The Three Little Pigs*, and have each person write a version with an alternate ending. Compare your stories when you're done.

- Watch a movie.
- Play each other's favorite video games.
- Ask each other silly and serious questions.

SILLY AND SERIOUS QUESTIONS

- How's your family?
- What's your best/worst class in school?
- What do you want to do when you grow up?
- If you could be anyone in the world, who would it be and why?
- What's the best sport?
- Ketchup or mustard on hot dogs?
- What's your favorite Bible story?
- Where do you want to travel?
- What are you doing this summer (or spring/winter break)?
- If you starred in a TV show, what would it be?
- What's your favorite talent?
- What's your favorite kind of cookie?
- What are you afraid of?

Next level: Hold a mega gaming contest! Track scores or wins and losses for each game you play. At the end of the twenty-four hours, the friend with the most points wins.

175

USE YOUR TALENTS!

"His master said to him, 'Well done, good and faithful servant. You have been faithful over a little; I will set you over much. Enter into the joy of your master.'"
—MATTHEW 25:21

When Justin and I started our YouTube channel in 2011, we did it just for fun, to make each other laugh. As we posted more videos, more people started seeing them and laughing too. We felt inspired to pursue a vision that we call "Laugh Daily," producing videos that bring joy to people's lives.

Our video-making skills have definitely grown since we began our journey. We've learned a lot about storytelling, editing, thumbnail designs, retention, and much more. But at our core, the goal is still to make people laugh. It's one of the main ways we serve God.

In Matthew 25, Jesus told a parable about using your gifts to serve the Lord. Like a master who puts his servants in charge while he's away, God has given each of us different gifts and abilities to use until Jesus' return. He wants us to use them to build His kingdom, bringing Him glory and doing good to others.

What are you good at? Is it math, science, music, painting, sports, or even whistling through your nose? Are you a natural-born leader? Are you better serving behind-the-scenes? Do you have a special place in your heart for people who are hurting? Whatever your gifts and abilities are, look for ways to use them. When you do that, you bring honor to God while helping others.

God wants you to develop your talents, just like the wise servants did in Jesus' parable. Talents don't do any good if you keep them hidden. You've got to use them.

Perhaps you haven't found your special talent yet. That's okay. Pray about it and start trying new things. You never know what God will start doing in you and through you.

In Jesus' parable, when the master returned, he praised and blessed his faithful servants, but he had only harsh words and judgment for the foolish servant who squandered his talents. This is a picture of what will happen when Jesus returns. The better choice is clear!

Don't waste your talents. Use them in ways big and small to be a light to others in a dark world. Then, when you stand before God face-to-face, you'll hear those amazing words from Him: "Well done, good and faithful servant. Enter into the joy of your master."

—ANDREW

AN EYE TOWARD OTHERS

Do nothing from selfish ambition or conceit, but in humility count others more significant than yourselves. Let each of you look not only to his own interests, but also to the interests of others.
—PHILIPPIANS 2:3–4

Have you ever performed a small act of kindness for someone? Maybe you've held the door open, complimented a friend's project, or offered to help a neighbor with yard work for free. Little gestures like these can make a big impact on people.

We turned this concept into a video and had a blast going around town spreading simple acts of kindness. In one instance, we placed a bouquet of flowers on a random car in a grocery store parking lot. As we waited with anticipation, the stranger returned to their car with a mix of surprise and confusion, excited that they had received a mysterious gift that brightened their day.

We are called to live focused on serving others. It's easy to get caught up in self-centered thinking because, after all, we're with ourselves 100 percent of the time. However, when we shift our focus to others, we open ourselves to the incredible opportunity to impact and bless people around us. It is truly better to give than to receive, as Jesus said. That idea really sunk in during that video.

Acts of kindness don't have to be grand. Even the small, simple things can have a significant impact.

Jesus is the perfect example of living an others-focused life. In Mark 10:45, He said that He "came not to be served but to serve" (NLT). Healing the sick, feeding the hungry, and loving the unlovable were just a few of the ways Jesus demonstrated His love. His ultimate act of self-sacrifice was dying on the cross to offer us the forgiveness of sins that we could never achieve on our own.

Jesus' life should inspire us to live lives of service and kindness to others. Because He sacrificed Himself for us, we should make sacrifices for others.

Today, take a moment to think creatively about how you can serve those around you, whether it's your family, friends, neighbors, or even a stranger. When you give your time and efforts to help someone else, you are modeling Jesus to them. His love should be the driving force. Your acts of kindness—through His power—have the ability to make a lasting difference in someone's life.

— JUSTIN

ACTS OF KINDNESS DON'T HAVE TO BE GRAND.

GO FOR IT!

Never be lazy, but work hard and serve the Lord enthusiastically.
—ROMANS 12:11 NLT

When I was younger, my family and I enjoyed watching the TV show *American Idol*. My favorite moments were the performances by less-than-stellar singers—you know, the ones who think they're nailing it, but in reality their voices were breaking glass somewhere offstage. Those moments always brought a good laugh.

We all have passions, but sometimes we're not exactly a natural at the thing that gets us excited. Can you relate to that? I know I can. God has gifted each of us with unique interests and abilities, not just for our benefit but for His glory and the good of others. He wants you to pursue your passions and lean into the gifts He's given you. But as you do, it's important to keep your focus on Him.

If you have a dream, go for it! Don't worry if you don't excel at it right away. After all, Beethoven, Picasso, and Maya Angelou weren't masters of their crafts immediately. They worked at them, sharpening and refining their God-given skills over time.

Personally, I've always been drawn to cameras—not so much the technical aspects, but being in front of them. There's an indescribable joy that fills me when the camera is recording. When I first pursued this interest, I started improving and feeling more comfortable with being in front of the camera. And now that passion supports a family. Who knew?

But even as I'm having a blast in front of the camera, I try to remember to keep my focus on bringing honor to God. No matter how funny I am on-screen or how great a video turns out, none of it matters if my heart isn't set on Him. God doesn't care if I look cool or if the video is super popular. He looks at our hearts—the motivation behind our efforts—and our faith. Why are we doing what we do? Are we focusing more on the gift, our glory, or the Giver of all things?

When we shift our focus from magnifying our abilities to the God who gave them to us, our perspective changes. Then we'll start pursuing our passions for the right reasons and be the best version of ourselves. It's all about using our unique talents to point back to Him.

As you pursue your interests and abilities, remember their origin and acknowledge that a gracious God has entrusted them to you. Then go out there and do your best in all things—all for the glory of God!

—JUSTIN

INNER DRIVE

> **Train yourself for godliness; for while bodily training is of some value, godliness is of value in every way, as it holds promise for the present life and also for the life to come.**
> —1 TIMOTHY 4:7–8

Everyone loves a game of capture the flag! As kids, we all played it at school and in our neighborhoods. But here at JStu, we love doing things on another level, so we played a twenty-four-hour game of capture the flag across the entire city of Denver! Four teams of four guys each spread out across town, using Airbnb rental houses for our bases. The prize for the winning team? The highly coveted title of Capture the Flag All-Time Champions—and a whopping $10,000!

It was one of the most amazing competitions I've ever been part of, filled with so many intense moments and adrenaline boosts. Each team wanted to win so badly. And after twenty-four hours, the last team standing was—well, go watch the video!

Everyone has an inner drive that pushes them forward. Even if you're not a highly competitive person, God has still given you different skills and interests you want to pursue. We put time, effort, and training into our passions, hoping to achieve great things.

In all this, what matters most is our motivation—the reason

behind our efforts. Those drives can be healthy or unhealthy. Striving for earthly goals has some value, but pursuing the kinds of goals God wants for us exceeds all other motivations because the rewards are eternal. Are you training, striving, and competing for temporary glory or for the eternal things of God?

Working hard to be the best at what you do is perfectly fine, but doing it for selfish reasons and personal recognition is not the right approach. Ultimately, it doesn't matter how many flags you capture, basketball games you win, or trophies you earn. What matters is how you treat others as you play and who you're giving the glory to.

As you train, strive, and compete, desire above all to win in your walk with God! Training for God goals involves seeking Him daily in prayer, Scripture reading, and hanging out with other Christians.

All the trophies and medals you win will eventually fade away. So strive for what truly matters—the forever-blessings of a life that's pleasing to God!

—ANDREW

EYE ON THE PRIZE

I press on to reach the end of the race and receive the heavenly prize for which God, through Christ Jesus, is calling us.
—PHILIPPIANS 3:14 NLT

Racing is one of my favorite things to do. I ran track and cross-country in high school, and one year our cross-country team placed second at the state championships. As a senior, I was named captain of the team, which included a lot of fun duties like cheering on the junior varsity runners.

But honestly, practice was kind of boring to me. Because I wasn't able to run at my top speeds during practice, I'd get frustrated and fall behind the pack, looking like an average racer. But when race day came, I'd turn on the jets again!

That's because a prize was on the line. Competition fueled me. My eye was always on finishing first and qualifying for the state championship, which I did three years in a row. Knowing what I was racing for made it easier to go all in and run as fast as I could.

Every race has a finish line. The goal is to cross that finish line and do it well, reaching whatever personal goal you've set. Remembering the end goal and the prize—whatever it might be—is important in athletics. And it's absolutely essential in Christianity.

As he occasionally did in his letters to first-century churches, the apostle Paul used racing to show what our ultimate motivation should be as followers of Jesus. In Philippians 3:14, he described life as a long race, with the goal being "the heavenly prize" of spending eternity with our Savior.

Life is definitely like a long cross-country race. It's filled with many twists and turns, hills and valleys—all followed by a glorious finish line. But unlike a normal cross-country race, where only a few top athletes receive a prize, every Christian who faithfully crosses the finish line of life will receive rewards beyond belief. Eternity in God's presence is by far the best prize imaginable!

Near the end of his life, Paul looked forward to crossing the finish line and receiving his eternal reward. In 2 Timothy 4:7, he wrote, "I have fought the good fight, *I have finished the race*, I have kept the faith" (emphasis added).

Don't walk, lazily jog, or give up on the race set before you. Keep your eyes on Jesus, and run hard toward the finish line!

— ANDREW

RUN HARD TOWARD JESUS.

THE JSTU OLYMPICS

Are you ready to be the best? Host your own JStu Olympics with your friends to see who's the best at some highly technical and athletically sophisticated events: crab walking, one-legged hopping, cracker eating, and more! Or make up your own events. The main goal is to get outside, have fun, and enjoy time with friends.

Let the JStu Olympics begin!

RULES

- Have fun.
- Laugh often.
- Keep score if you want.
- Be a good sport.
- Don't end up in the hospital.

SCORING

Each person receives a score for each event.

  First place = 15 points

  Second place = 10 points

  Third place = 5 points

Choose a prize for the person who finishes all events with the most points.

EVENTS

1. **Sprint**—Who's the fastest from the starting line to the finish line?
2. **Object throw**—Who can throw an object the farthest (a football, a baseball, someone's shoe, or a water balloon)?
3. **Cracker-eating**—Who can eat the most saltine crackers in a minute (with no water breaks)?
4. **Long jump**—With a running start, who can jump the farthest from the starting line? Mark where each competitor lands (with a foot, hand, or any other flailing body part).
5. **Running backward**—Who is the fastest at running backward?
6. **Push-ups**—Who can do the most push-ups in a minute?
7. **One-legged hop**—Who is the fastest at hopping on one leg?
8. **Frisbee throw**—Who can throw a Frisbee closest to a marker?
9. **Crab walk**—Who can crab walk the fastest?
10. **Staring**—Who can stare at another contestant the longest without laughing? No touching allowed, but goofy faces and ridiculous noises are encouraged!

Next level: The winner of the Olympic decathlon is called "the World's Greatest Athlete." Raise the stakes in your JStu Olympics with bragging rights. The champion will win the right to be called "the Greatest Athlete" or another title of your creation by every other competitor for a week.

YOU CAN'T TAKE IT WITH YOU

"Do not lay up for yourselves treasures on earth, where moth and rust destroy and where thieves break in and steal, but lay up for yourselves treasures in heaven, where neither moth nor rust destroys and where thieves do not break in and steal."
—MATTHEW 6:19–20

The JStu team is always looking for new equipment and the latest technology to help with our YouTube channel. In 2023, we found a new drone that was perfect for our needs. After a few practice runs with it, we set out to film a video on a lake.

For the video, Justin and I were going to spend the night sailing in a micro yacht that our team built. (And if you're wondering what a micro yacht is, well, picture a floating vessel barely big enough for two people that's powered by bicycle pedals. Hey, nobody said we were trying to win a major boat race here!)

About halfway through our yachting adventure, we launched the drone to get some *sick* shots. Unfortunately, it crashed into the lake, never to be seen again. And we lost all the footage. (I won't say who did it, but his first name starts with *J* and ends with *ustin*. But again, not pointing fingers or anything.) When we called Rick, our tech expert, to share the bad news, he replied, "That breaks my heart a little bit. That thing was hard to get."

Such is life. Some days you get amazing aerial shots to enhance your videos, and other days your super-cool drone—and a big chunk of money—sinks in a lake.

Our drone debacle was a stark reminder that nothing in this life lasts forever. Money runs out. Possessions get old, break, and are lost. Gear crashes. And we can't take any of it to heaven. Anyone who puts their efforts into piling up wealth and possessions will ultimately be disappointed.

Humans are sight- and touch-oriented, but we need to reorient our minds to think beyond the physical (Colossians 3:2). We live in a spiritual realm where authentic treasures are the ones you can't lose in a lake. They're spiritual blessings that last forever.

Shifting your perspective to prioritize spiritual treasure doesn't come naturally. It requires prayer, time reading about God's perspective in Scripture, and patience. But with God's help, we can learn to pursue the things that truly matter—things we often can't see.

To store up treasures in heaven, our desires must be set on God. This is what Jesus was getting at when He said, "Where your treasure is, there your heart will be also" (Matthew 6:21). We need to value and pursue what God values—things like love, faith, kindness, mercy, peace, and patience. When we do this, we build treasures in heaven.

Earthly stuff is fun and helpful. God has given us clothes, video games, sports gear, cool tech—and yeah, even expensive drones—to enjoy but not to worship. So set your heart on God and His purposes in this life, and you'll be greatly rewarded in the next!

—ANDREW

ONLY ONE

"No one can serve two masters, for either he will hate the one and love the other, or he will be devoted to the one and despise the other. You cannot serve God and money."
—MATTHEW 6:24

Making money isn't easy. It often *takes* money to *make* money. So you can imagine how tough it would be to increase your wealth when you start out with a single penny.

That was the challenge Andrew and I took on for one of our videos. Armed with one cent each, we competed to see who could accumulate the most money in a twenty-four-hour period. And let me tell you, it was hard!

I did chores for my parents, bought lottery tickets, and attempted to sell random stuff to strangers. It didn't turn out the way I had planned (shocker!), and I spent the entire twenty-four hours stressed and rushing around, solely focused on the pursuit of money.

While this challenge was harmless fun, it highlights a truth that deserves our attention: we are called to serve God as our master, not material wealth. As I ran around town fixated on the relentless pursuit of money for our video, it was challenging to engage in anything truly meaningful. The pursuit of money ultimately leaves us spiritually bankrupt.

Money can bring temporary happiness, but it'll eventually fade away. Sure, it can help you buy a big house, a sweet car, or high-end clothes, but it can't draw you closer to God. It can't purchase a rich community of family and friends. And as the old saying goes, "You can't take it with you."

In and of itself, money isn't wrong. It can help with life's necessities, but even then, we need to remember that God is our ultimate Provider, not money.

In Matthew 6:24, Jesus warned about the dangers of chasing after material things. It's simply not possible for our hearts to fully pursue God and material wealth. We have to choose between the two.

At the end of our video, my grand total was $145.33. Not bad considering what I started with. But if you do the math, that's only about $6 an hour. I made more money at my first afterschool job in high school!

What's your relationship with money and material possessions? How do you view these things in light of your relationship with God? If you want to truly be rich, pursue the love of God and others. Prioritize Him and you'll discover a true treasure that far exceeds $145.33—or any amount!

— JUSTIN

THE PURSUIT OF MONEY ULTIMATELY LEAVES US SPIRITUALLY BANKRUPT.

IN HIS HANDS

> "Do not be anxious about your life, what you will eat or what you will drink, nor about your body, what you will put on. Is not life more than food, and the body more than clothing?"
>
> —MATTHEW 6:25

Most of our videos are so much fun to film that I wish they'd last longer. But one in particular I couldn't wait to end! That would be our "Extreme Survival House" video, in which Andrew, Isaac, and I were trapped in a house of horrors.

The house featured one hundred mystery buttons. Only by pressing the right one could we escape. As for the other ninety-nine? Well, each of those represented a looming disaster.

Before we finally escaped, we had to endure a tsunami, hurricane, mudslide, blizzard, sandstorm, tornado, heat wave, worm invasion, nuke attack—shall I go on? It was hilarious and absolutely awful. I learned that day that some of our team members who came up with the disasters are more heartless than I realized!

One of the worst parts of the challenge—other than, you know, being covered in some of the worst substances on planet earth—was not knowing what was coming next. Isn't that true of life in general? Even when it doesn't involve buckets of worms being dumped on your head, life is full of uncertainties and unexpected twists. All the cares of life—even down to our basic needs like food, shelter, and clothing—can start to shoot up our worry meter.

But worrying shows a lack of trust in God. When we worry, it's like telling God that the issue we're facing is too big for Him to handle. And that's just not true.

Jesus spoke about these things in Matthew 6, giving us loving reassurance about our supreme worth to God. He said that God feeds the birds and clothes the flowers—things in creation that aren't nearly as important as human beings—and He will certainly take care of all our needs too (Matthew 6:26–30).

Our response to the cares of life should be trust. God will meet all our needs—and so much more! Look around, my friend. From the smallest critters to the most majestic mountains, everything in creation is a reminder of God's provision. He's *got* you.

Life is full of unknowns—especially when you're trapped in an extreme survival house and desperately needing a long, hot shower. But each step of the way, God will provide for all your needs.

— JUSTIN

SOMETHING'S GOT TO GIVE

Whoever sows sparingly will also reap sparingly, and whoever sows bountifully will also reap bountifully. Each one must give as he has decided in his heart, not reluctantly or under compulsion, for God loves a cheerful giver.

—2 CORINTHIANS 9:6–7

Over the years, we've done a number of videos where we've gone to a store and bought the entire stock of a particular item. So in October 2019, the natural evolution of this fun idea led us to our local Target store to buy every single—*wait for it . . . wait for it*—roll of toilet paper!

I'm not gonna lie. It was a *lot* of toilet paper. We cleared out the entire aisle and spent $5,000. We had so much TP that we had to rent a van to transport it back to our warehouse!

What was the point of this peculiar purchase? Why, to make a giant castle with it for a video, of course! Talk about bathroom humor. After we finished, we were stuck with a ridiculous amount of TP and didn't quite know what to do with it.

Five months later, the global COVID-19 pandemic hit, and guess what people were scrambling for—yep, toilet paper! While virtually every store in town seemed to be sold out, we had hundreds of rolls in reserve! So we loaded up our van and drove around town, handing out free toilet paper to people. Every recipient was so happy. Some even cried.

Only God could have orchestrated this. When we cleaned out Target's supply, we had no idea toilet paper would soon be worth more than gold. But God has a way of designing what we could never imagine, and we were happy to participate in His plan.

God loves a cheerful giver. He loves watching us give joyfully. Why? Because He has cheerfully given countless blessings to us, including the free gift of salvation through His Son, Jesus. He wants us to reflect His generous character.

You never know the impact that even a small act of generosity can have on a person. To you, it might just be some toilet paper. But to someone else, it might provide hope and meet an important need at a critical time. God has given so much to you. Find ways to reflect His character and be a giver today!

— ANDREW

DOES GOD NEED OUR MONEY?

Honor the LORD with your wealth and with the firstfruits of all your produce; then your barns will be filled with plenty, and your vats will be bursting with wine.

—PROVERBS 3:9–10

We go to great lengths to protect our money. Our online bank accounts are encrypted and password protected. Banks store money in heavily secured vaults and transfer it in armored vehicles with armed guards. There's even such a thing as an armored piggy bank!

Justin, Samuel, and I found this out while filming a budget challenge to see who could break into an armored piggy bank containing $1,000. The first guy to break into the piggy bank got to keep the money!

The contraption looked like an actual oversized piggy bank, but it was made with bulletproof glass and super-thick metal. Bet you didn't have one of those when you were little!

From sledgehammers to skid-steer loaders, we tried all sorts of ways to break into that crazy pig! Let's just say that in a contest between the piggy bank and flying cinder blocks, Power Piggy wins every time.

As we consider the proper place of money in our lives, it's important to remember this: all our earthly possessions are ultimately gifts from God, and He wants us to give a portion of our money back to Him. Why does the Ruler of the universe ask us to do this? Is God a little short on cash? Does He need it to pay the rent or keep the lights on in heaven?

No!

God doesn't need anything, including our money. Our all-powerful God is 100 percent self-sufficient. But He *does* want our trust. He knows our hearts are inclined to trust in things other than Him, including money. He wants us to worship Him alone, to give our best to Him, and to serve others. Giving a portion of our money to God accomplishes all this!

In His wisdom, He chooses to use our money to bless others and increase our reliance on Him. For example, when you give money to a church, they might use those funds to pay hardworking staff, run programs that help people in the community, and support missionaries. In this way, God invites you to join Him in building His kingdom!

Some of your money *with* God's blessing actually goes further than all of your money *without* God's blessing. So break open your piggy bank and give joyfully to the Lord. He will provide for all your needs and bless you in ways that are far more valuable than your cash.

—ANDREW

24-Hour True Treasure Hunt

During our earning challenge, we worked super hard, but what we earned wasn't very much considering all the time and effort we put in. That just goes to show that chasing money doesn't get you very far.

Now it's your turn, but let's add a twist! Instead of earning money for yourself (what a waste!), raise money for charity. That way you can turn a little bit of cash into true treasure for someone in need.

RULES

1. You have twenty-four hours to complete the challenge.
2. Start with one cent.
3. Follow all laws, school rules, and family rules as you earn.
4. Do not go into anyone's house unless you have permission from your parent or guardian.
5. Choose a charity and give away your full earnings.

CHARITY IDEAS

- animal shelter
- women and children's shelter
- foster care organization
- Compassion International
- Samaritan's Purse
- library
- Operation Gratitude
- Special Olympics

MONEY-MAKING IDEAS

- Ask for donations.
- Do chores or yard work for family members and neighbors.
- Buy popular snacks and sell them at a higher price.
- Hold a bake sale.
- Do a lemonade stand if it's warm or a hot chocolate stand if it's cold.
- Walk a neighbor's dog.
- Teach an adult how to do something on their computer or phone.
- Sell some of your old clothes or toys at a consignment shop.
- Make and sell artwork, jewelry, T-shirts, or another product.
- Hold a car wash.
- Collect recyclables and take them to a center that pays for them.
- Babysit.

SELF-CARE, SOUL-CARE

> Do you not know that your body is a temple of the Holy Spirit within you, whom you have from God? You are not your own, for you were bought with a price. So glorify God in your body.
> —1 CORINTHIANS 6:19–20

When I turned thirty, I decided to make a change for my body. I wanted to take fitness more seriously and become stronger than I had ever been. So I hired a personal trainer and started an individual workout routine.

You only get one body on this earth, so it's important to treat it well. Physical exercise is a great way to do that. But according to the Bible, your body is more than just a collection of muscles and physical matter. If you are a follower of Jesus, your body is a temple of the Holy Spirit!

Now, you might be thinking, *Sounds interesting. But what in the world does that mean?* Glad you asked!

In ancient Israel, the temple was the sacred building in Jerusalem where the Jews worshipped God. Just as God once placed His presence inside that temple, He now places His presence—the Holy Spirit—inside every Christian. Think about how incredible that is. When God says He is always with us, it's true! His Spirit actually dwells inside us.

Knowing this should inform how we treat our bodies. If God's Spirit lives inside you, there can be no greater motivation to take care of your body! This includes the food you eat, the media you watch and listen to, the choices you make about safety, and much more.

For many of us, our body doesn't feel much like a sacred temple. Some people have bodies that struggle with illnesses. Others have limitations such as physical disabilities or allergies. But remember, your body isn't a temple because of how it looks or what it can or can't do. Your body deserves honor because of the One who lives inside it.

So if the gym is your thing, pound out those burpees, bench presses, and bicep curls. But if that's not your vibe, don't sweat it. You don't have to look like Dwayne "The Rock" Johnson to glorify God with your body. God just wants you to honor Him in the body choices you make.

You were bought with a price. All of you: your mind, body, and soul. And that price was God's Son, Jesus. So honor God with your body!

—ANDREW

YOUR BODY DESERVES HONOR BECAUSE THE HOLY SPIRIT LIVES INSIDE IT.

GARBAGE IN, GARBAGE OUT

Do not be deceived: God is not mocked, for whatever one sows, that will He also reap.
—GALATIANS 6:7

There's an old saying: "Garbage in, garbage out." It's pretty self-explanatory. If you put junk in your body, junk will come out of your body. That was certainly true during our "One Hundred Chicken Nuggets Challenge" video!

This video featured my brother's three college roommates, who were all confident they could eat one hundred Chicken McNuggets from McDonald's in one sitting. When we ordered three hundred nuggets at our local McDonald's, the staff thought we were pranking them.

Holding the challenge in my kitchen, we broke it down into ten-nugget rounds, with various challenges and prizes on the line. The guys started off strong in round one. Round two was a little more difficult. And when they had several dozen nuggets in their bellies, that's when the puking started. Let's just say the guys' digestive systems—and my backyard—took a beating that day.

Garbage in, garbage out—it's true with McNuggets, and it's just as true with our spiritual lives. Galatians 6:7 puts it another way, in agricultural terms: You reap what you sow. If a farmer plants good seeds, he'll get a good crop. If he sows worthless seeds, he'll get weeds in return.

It's important to avoid putting anything in your body that dishonors God and is harmful to you either physically, mentally, or spiritually. This certainly includes things that will cause you physical harm like drugs, smoking, and excessive amounts of junk food. But it also includes what you see in movies, what you hear in music, and what you read on social media.

God made you and loves you greatly! He wants you to take care of your body. So be mindful of what you allow into it in all respects. Putting the garbage of things like inappropriate movies, tasteless video games, unwholesome internet content, and profanity-laced music into your mind can lead to garbage coming out—anger, pride, foul language, poor self-image, a harmful view of others, and more.

Instead, fill your mind with good, spiritually uplifting things—most of all, the Word of God! The more you digest Scripture, the healthier a person you'll be!

So remember: garbage in, garbage out. You reap what you sow. It's a nugget of wisdom that will serve you well.

— ANDREW

THE EYE TEST

**I will not set before my eyes
anything that is worthless.**
—PSALM 101:3

Our eyes are truly remarkable! They grant us the ability to behold vibrant colors, perceive depths, and navigate the world around us each day.

Throughout my life, I've been blessed with incredible experiences, from scuba diving among exotic fish in South Africa, to skydiving over the Alps in Switzerland, to visiting an active volcano in Iceland. I wouldn't have been able to fully appreciate all these marvels without the gift of sight.

However, in the midst of creation's visual wonders, great darkness is also around us too. Sin permeates our surroundings, presenting itself through inappropriate scenes on our screens, explicit content on social media, suggestive billboards on our roadways, and much more. It's vital for us to guard our eyes from these harmful influences. Andrew touched on this in yesterday's "garbage in, garbage out" devotion, but today we're going to focus specifically on honoring God with what we look at.

God calls us to holiness. That means He wants us to set ourselves apart from the sinful lures that lead us away from Him. This may be challenging because there are all kinds of ungodly images all around us. But here's the good news: God equips believers with the Holy Spirit to help us in moments of temptation and struggle. Led by the Spirit, we can make conscious choices to look away from what is harmful and fix our eyes on what's good and pure.

In our weakness, God's strength shines through. By immersing ourselves in His Word, seeking His help in prayer, and pursuing accountability with fellow believers, we can guard ourselves against the snares of the enemy. Instead of dwelling on the darkness of this world, let's fix our gaze on the splendor of God's holiness, grace, and love toward us in Jesus.

Remember to be intentional about what you look at. Be vigilant about what captures your attention. Let your eyes be receptors of God's light and goodness, reflecting His glory to those around you.

In God's strength, you have the power to overcome, to see His beauty amid the darkness, and to walk in the freedom of His love.

— JUSTIN

No TROLLING

Let no corrupting talk come out of your mouths, but only such as is good for building up, as fits the occasion, that it may give grace to those who hear.
—EPHESIANS 4:29

Every parent tells their kids not to talk to strangers. But truth be told, talking to strangers was the backbone of our early JStu videos. Sorry, Mom and Dad.

In one video years ago, Justin and I sucked on helium balloons before placing our orders at a local fast-food drive-thru. Sounding like crazy high-pitched chipmunks, we made up wild stories to make the staff laugh. In one scene, I pretended to be a grandpa taking my grandson for a ride in a Cadillac as we searched for football trading cards. The lady at the drive-thru window couldn't keep it together, and I cracked up too because I sounded insane and the story made no sense.

You don't need cars, lighter-than-air gas, and a drive-thru to make an impact with your words. Proverbs 18:21 says, "Death and life are in the power of the tongue." Your words can either tear people down or build them up.

Few things in life are more important than how you talk to others—your family members, teachers, classmates, friends, people who *aren't* your friends, everyone! Your words should be filled with encouragement, joy, and love, not with unkindness, bitterness, and anger.

This is just as true in how we speak online as it is when we talk in person. Whether you're texting a friend or leaving a comment on someone's Instagram post, remember that there's a human being on the other end of that message—someone made in God's image with feelings and emotions, just like you.

Your words have great power. Use them to help and heal, not to harm. Think before you speak and consider if what you want to say will honor God and be a blessing to others. With a gentle spirit and a heart that wants to put others first, you can be a powerful source of joy simply by the way you speak.

No helium required.

— ANDREW

> REMEMBER THERE'S A HUMAN BEING ON THE OTHER END OF EVERY MESSAGE.

THE REAL THING

**Behold, how good and pleasant it is
when brothers dwell in unity!**
—PSALM 133:1

Let's talk about the love-hate relationship many of us have with social media.

For me, with over a decade (and counting) in the internet game, it's been an interesting ride of learning and, if I'm honest, a fair share of wasting time. Social media can either be your trusty sidekick in doing something awesome or a black hole where time vanishes without a trace.

A wise friend once told me that he doesn't follow friends online. He'd rather get the lowdown on their lives in person, not through pixels. I understand where he's coming from. Friendships can be delicate matters, and social media is a tricky business. It's easy for people to be something they're not online. Relationships can only go so far when people are connected mainly through screens. On the other hand, face-to-face chats with friends are the real deal. Your offline life is the true gold mine.

Psalm 133:1 talks about the goodness of friends enjoying time together. It's not talking about surviving one hundred hours in an underground bunker together, JStu-style. It's talking about pursuing real, heart-to-heart connections with other people who share a similar faith and value system as yours.

Let's face it: hitting the "like" button is not the definition of a meaningful friendship, and it's about as exciting as watching ice melt. But looking a friend in the eye, enjoying laughs together, and sharing your victories and losses side by side—now *that*'s powerful. Those are the kinds of deep connections God made us for.

Jesus gave us lots of examples of building meaningful relationships during His time on earth. He intentionally sought twelve men (and others) and invested deeply in them through conversation and time together. He spent much of His three-year earthly ministry in their company, and look what it produced! Because of their intimate friendship with Jesus, some of these men wrote New Testament books—detailed accounts of Jesus' life, death, resurrection, and ascension—and other God-inspired letters. After Jesus returned to heaven, His friends spread the good news of His resurrection and the offer of salvation throughout the Roman Empire, forever changing the world. And it's all because Jesus spent time with His friends, teaching them to dwell in unity.

Don't let social media hijack your friendship priorities. Pause the scroll, call a friend, and make some awesome memories. We were made for authentic, in-person relationships with others. Your offline, in-person friendships are where the good stuff happens. So unplug and go hang!

— JUSTIN

7-DAY DETOX

The daily mission of a Jesus follower is essentially to replace bad with good. Out with negative thoughts, in with gratitude. Out with selfishness, in with putting God first.

This challenge is all about being, doing, and feeling better. Let's do it!

DAY 1: REPLACE JUNK FOOD WITH A HEALTHY SNACK.

Pump real energy into your body by having a smoothie or salad for a snack.

> **Pro tip:** Frozen fruit makes a smoothie thicker, colder, and more refreshing.

DAY 2: REPLACE MESSAGING WITH HANG-OUT TIME.

Meet up with a pal in person. You'll have a great time, create memories, and strengthen your friendship in ways you simply can't do through a screen.

DAY 3: REPLACE SCROLLING WITH SCRIPTURE.

Take a twenty-four-hour social media break, and spend some solid time in God's Word.

DAY 4: BE POSITIVE ON SOCIAL MEDIA.

Add positivity and encouragement to your feed.

- Share a Bible verse and what it means to you.
- Post encouraging comments on your friends' pages or posts.
- If you see a negative post, respond with something positive (but not preachy!).
- Share a link to a cool upcoming church or community event.

DAY 5: REPLACE GAMING WITH YOU TIME.

Chill out in your own way. Draw, play an instrument or listen to music, read a book, or take a walk. Take a break from your noisy, busy life to just hang out, think, and be you.

DAY 6: REPLACE COMPLAINING WITH GRATITUDE.

Want to see your parent's or teacher's eyes bug out like space aliens'? Write a thank-you note for how they help you in life.

DAY 7: REPLACE TECH WITH EXERCISE.

Give your body and mind a boost with physical activity!

- Take a walk or jog.
- Go for a swim.
- Go for a ride on your bike, scooter, skateboard, unicycle, pogo stick, Shetland pony—whatever.
- Gather friends to play a sport or capture the flag.

Next level: Try this exercise routine:

1. 20 jumping jacks
2. 10 push-ups
3. 10 sit-ups
4. 5 squats
5. 5 burpees
6. 2-minute cool-down walk

THE CHOICE IS YOURS

> Trust in the LORD with all your heart, and do not lean on your own understanding. In all your ways acknowledge him, and he will make straight your paths.
> —PROVERBS 3:5–6

Have you ever done something truly dumb?

Over the years, we have made plenty of poor decisions in our JStu videos. Pick any budget challenge, and you'll probably see one of us trying to make something out of nothing, usually resulting in a minor catastrophe.

Take our ultimate overnight survival challenge. Wanting a cool vibe, Isaac set up a firepit outside his shelter, which was sitting on an artificial outdoor rug. It seemed like a nice touch, but soon we noticed an unusual smell. The intense heat from the firepit was burning a hole through the rug below! We quickly put out the fire, avoided any serious damage, and had some good laughs.

We're all faced with many decisions in life. Our choices are important, both for our relationship with God and our relationships with others.

God has given you plenty of intelligence, but we're all capable of some real dumb decisions, no matter who you are! A big reason for this is our sinful natures. We all have a natural tendency toward pride, selfishness, impatience, and anger. These sins often conspire to affect our judgment and produce some really bad choices. But there's a better way.

To make the best decisions in life, we need to rely on the Author of life Himself. God has all wisdom, knowledge, and power. Trusting in His wisdom rather than our own ideas is always the way to go.

The Bible is a road map for life. Whenever you're faced with a fork in the road, God's Word will point you in the right direction. The more time you spend reading the Bible and praying for understanding, the more equipped you'll be to make good choices. God will make your paths straight, meaning your decisions will become clearer. When your thoughts, intentions, and actions are aligned with God's heart, it's easy to see His way.

The Bible won't give you the specific answer for every choice you need to make. It won't tell you what to have for breakfast tomorrow, what sport to play, or what to study in college. But even when it doesn't give detailed instructions, the Bible always gives principles that you can use to guide your choices.

God has given you the tools you need for good decision-making. So avoid the disastrous firepit of prideful, selfish thinking, and seek God's wisdom! He's set you up for success.

— ANDREW

HONESTY IS THE BEST POLICY

A man who makes a vow to the LORD or makes a pledge under oath must never break it. He must do exactly what he said he would do.
—NUMBERS 30:2 NLT

What do you think would happen if you strapped yourself and your friends to a lie detector test and asked some very personal questions? Things would get real crazy real quick! Ask me how I know. . . .

With our JStu team members watching the interrogation room through one-way glass, Andrew and I faced a barrage of challenging questions—the kind that make you squirm. We had to answer probing inquiries such as "Who is your favorite employee?" and "Who would be the first person you'd fire?" and even "Would you betray a team member for $6 million?" These were tough questions, and our friends had a blast putting us on the spot. The lie detector revealed some pretty fascinating truths—and a few fibs!

Thankfully, we don't walk around each day connected to lie detectors. But our honesty is still super important! The Bible is very clear on the importance of truth-telling and promise-keeping.

God is the source and definition of all truth. And He calls each of us to reflect His character in this way. It all boils down to living a life of integrity—that means being someone others can trust.

After all, if others can't trust you in your words or actions, what else do you have in life? Few things are more important than being honest and trustworthy.

In the moment, it can be easy to think, *No one's going to know if I lie. So what harm can it do?* But the truth has a funny way of surfacing—even when you're not hooked up to a nerve-wracking polygraph machine! And even if no one else finds out about your lie, God knows. He knows the thoughts and intentions of our hearts (Psalm 139:1–3). There's no fooling God.

So the next time you're faced with a truth-dodging dilemma, remember that God calls you to integrity for your good, the good of your relationships with others, and His glory.

Telling the truth isn't always easy. But the long-term payoff is always better than the consequences of dishonesty. Let's be the crew that strives for integrity even when it gets tricky. When we choose truth, we're giving a shout-out to the One who has always been truthful to us!

—JUSTIN

GOD IS THE SOURCE AND DEFINITION OF ALL TRUTH.

STANDING STRONG

We aim at what is honorable not only in the Lord's sight but also in the sight of man.

—2 CORINTHIANS 8:21

We have filmed countless videos in college libraries over the years. Most students go there to either take study notes or review them. So we thought it would make a funny video if we tried to copy people's notes but with a JStu twist. The gag was that we'd make it ridiculously obvious that we were trying to cheat, but as soon as the person noticed, we'd act like we weren't doing anything wrong.

Some of our fake-cheating methods were over-the-top—literally. In one scene, I awkwardly reached over a guy's shoulder to take photos of his notes with my phone—with the camera sound effect volume turned on high! In another scene, I stood behind a fake plant, hidden from absolutely no one, and pretended to peek over someone's shoulder. Most people were confused and some even shared their notes with us, even though we didn't actually need them.

Our video was just for kicks. There was no real cheating involved. But here's a real-life truth: whether in public or private, followers of Jesus are to show integrity at all times. Integrity is simply being honest and choosing to do what's right, whether people are watching or not. You should aim for integrity with God and with other people, no matter what's going on.

Integrity builds trust. Showing integrity with your friends displays your love for them. Everyone wants friends they can trust, so be that person!

Showing integrity isn't always easy. You'll be faced with situations where being honorable might put an unwanted spotlight on you as you stand up for what's right. But between doing what's right and following the crowd, integrity is always the right choice.

Being honorable in private is just as important as it is in public. Even if no one else can see what you're doing, God can. And His judgment matters most. So be honest with Him. And if you create habits of integrity in private, you'll be much better equipped when you face tough decisions in public.

Blatantly fake-cheating behind fake plants for a few video laughs is one thing. But real-life integrity is no joke! Make integrity with people and God a habit.

— ANDREW

HOW TEMPTING!

No temptation has overtaken you that is not common to man. God is faithful, and he will not let you be tempted beyond your ability, but with the temptation he will also provide the way of escape, that you may be able to endure it.

–1 CORINTHIANS 10:13

I really didn't mean to shatter glass all over poor Isaac's head. Honest!

In our "Stranded 100 Hours in a Survival Bunker" video, I noticed Isaac was sitting underneath a piece of framed artwork on the wall. I also noticed it was barely hanging on one little nail, and that with any disturbance, the artwork would fall on Isaac's head.

What would you have done in my shoes?

I didn't want to hurt Isaac, but hey, sometimes minor pain can be funny. So I gave into the temptation, hit the wall, and the picture bonked his head. Shards went everywhere.

Oops.

Had I thought about it a little more, I probably wouldn't have sent that picture crashing down. But I just knew it would be hilarious.

Dealing with temptation is tough! God has given us important rules to follow in His Word. These are for our own good and the good of others. But we often get tempted to break God's good rules. These temptations can come in all forms and sizes and at any time. They can be as silly as what I did to Isaac or much more serious, with longer-lasting consequences. The temptations themselves aren't sinful; what matters is whether we choose to give in to them or not.

Sin is tempting because it promises pleasure, fun, popularity, success, and more. But ultimately, giving in to temptation only delivers pain, difficulties, and a break in our relationship with God.

Here's the good news: God doesn't lay traps for us, and He will never allow a temptation in your life that you can't avoid. Whenever you're tempted, you can always choose to do the right thing. God always provides a way out. Every single time.

How is this possible? Because Jesus has gone before you and encountered every kind of temptation, except without sinning (Hebrews 4:15). And He gives you access to His power to resist temptation through God's Spirit, who lives inside every believer.

One of the best ways to resist temptation is to have a few key Bible verses memorized. Psalm 119:11 and Matthew 26:41 come to mind. When facing a strong temptation, meditate on God's Word, and it will help you set your thoughts on Him (Colossians 3:2).

Because you have an almighty God who loves you and a Savior who has defeated sin itself, you have the power to overcome every temptation through Jesus—including hilarious but harmful pranks on your friends.

— ANDREW

HIDE-AND-SEEK

If you need wisdom, ask our generous God, and he
will give it to you. He will not rebuke you for asking.

—JAMES 1:5 NLT

Ah, the classic game of hide-and-seek—the OG adrenaline rush!
As I was growing up, hide-and-seek was my absolute favorite game
to play. The thrill of tucking myself away to avoid detection or
trying to uncover all my friends' whereabouts was super fun.

Hide-and-seek isn't just for kids though. Right?

We decided to take the game to epic levels—one hundred
hours of hide-and-seek involving ten players and spanning the
entire state of Colorado! In our game, the seeker was equipped
with a GPS tracker and knew everyone else's locations at all times.
Anyone he caught instantly became a seeker too.

With a thirty-minute head start, the other hiders and I quickly
fanned out across the city—and further!—using bikes, Ubers, car
rentals, and more, as we competed for a $5,000 prize. Talk about
intensity! It was hide-and-seek on steroids!

Do you ever find yourself playing a hide-and-seek with God?
Whether it's in the daily choices we make or the wisdom we need,
we often forget God's presence, dive into our own spiritual hiding
spots, and rely on our own wisdom. That never ends well.

But God never hides from us. He's always right there, offering what we need. Need wisdom? Ask God and *boom*—it's yours. And get this: God doesn't play favorites. He generously hands out wisdom to everyone who asks. Wrap your head around that!

In our life-size game of hide-and-seek, the seeker knew our every move. But God's perfect knowledge is way better than any human GPS. As the God who knows and sees all, He's always tuned in to where you are—not just physically, but also emotionally and spiritually.

Are you feeling lost? Unsure? Confused about which way to go or what to do? There's no greater guide in life than God! Don't hide from the One with all the answers. Seek after Him. Trust in His wisdom, and pursue the life-giving truths in His Word.

Hiding from God can be a real stress fest, but in seeking Him and His wisdom, there's incredible relief in knowing you're in the right hands. And check this out: God is seeking you too! He wants to draw you near. So will you let yourself be found?

Today, ask God for wisdom wherever you need it, and watch as your old, frustrating game of hide-and-seek transforms into a super-cool wisdom treasure hunt. God's got the ultimate cheat codes, and you're in for an amazing revelation. Get ready to be found, my friend—God sees you right where you are!

—JUSTIN

BUILD YOUR OWN BUDGET CHALLENGE

Life is all about choices. As followers of Jesus, it's important that we make good choices each day according to God's Word. We at JStu make choices all the time, like when we use our Plinko board to randomly determine the amounts of money we can each spend on wacky budget challenges. So now it's time to play your own JStu-style budget challenge!

HOW TO PLAY

1. Decide what you'll do in your budget challenge (see suggestions).
2. Determine the budget amounts:
   • Each participant will contribute an equal amount. Decide what that amount is.
   • Add the contributions together to calculate the total you will have for the challenge. For example, if five participants are each contributing $10, you'll have $50 total.
   • Divide the total into amounts for each participant. You could divide your $50 total into five individual budgets of $20, $10, $8, $7, and $5.
3. Write the amounts on slips of paper, and put them in a cup. Take turns selecting your budget amount.
4. Let the challenge begin!

IDEAS

- Buy items to use for dares with the other participants. Need inspiration? Watch our "$5 vs. $250 Dares! Budget Challenge" video!
- Take the group out to eat.
- Make a meal or dessert.
- Make a gift for a holiday or birthday with items from a craft store.
- Throw a party.
- Build a backyard fort.

Next level: Build your own Plinko board to determine the budget amounts.

THE COST OF LOVE

Walk in love, as Christ loved us and gave himself up for us, a fragrant offering and sacrifice to God.
—EPHESIANS 5:2

It was time for another budget challenge! Andrew, Seth, and I dropped balls down the Plinko board, and my ball fell in the big kahuna—$4,000! But for this challenge we weren't heading to the store to buy supplies. We set out into the world to give it away and hopefully make a difference in some lives.

I had so much fun spending my money on others. I gave a waitress a crazy tip, provided a shopping spree for a random customer, and paid someone's rent. As my budget decreased, my joy skyrocketed. Perhaps my favorite moment was picking up one of our biggest fans from school, driving him and his mom home in the JStu ambulance, and surprising him with a ton of amazing toys we'd placed in his room.

Throughout the video, my smile remained as a constant companion. It's an incredible feeling when you show people love and kindness. It's a feeling that words can't capture. You just have to experience it!

Love always costs something. You can love others without spending any money, but it will always require sacrificing something of value. Loving others demands our time, energy, and resources.

I'm so glad we spent the day—and a chunk of cash—blessing others! Seeing the joy on those strangers' faces was well worth it. Better yet, we got to display the love of Jesus to them—a love far greater than any dollar figure.

There's no greater love than the sacrificial love of Jesus. His love for us cost His own life, given without expecting anything in return. His example is the perfect illustration of love in action. As you ponder how Jesus has loved us, consider how you can serve those around you, following in the footsteps of our Savior.

Serving isn't a chore. It's a privilege and an opportunity to make a positive impact. So embrace the joy of serving, knowing that every act of love, big and small, reflects the love of Jesus. Your sacrificial love can leave a lasting imprint on someone's heart. Challenge yourself to find ways to serve those around you, spreading the sacrificial love of Jesus wherever you go.

— JUSTIN

LOVE ALWAYS COSTS SOMETHING.

FIRST THINGS FIRST

He sat down and called the twelve. And he said to them, "If anyone would be first, he must be last of all and servant of all."

—MARK 9:35

Who doesn't love a good, old-fashioned road trip?

In 2022, Justin, Blake, and I did a video series of a road trip we took from Colorado to Chicago. The goal was to deliver a briefcase containing $5,000 to the nonprofit organization called Feeding America. Another YouTuber, Ryan Trahan, was doing a series for Feeding America, and we wanted to help and make it fun.

So we drove into the heartland in a camper van. But somewhere in Nebraska, our van broke down. SO we had to get the van towed to the nearest mechanic in a little farming town. They said it couldn't be fixed for about a week!

We couldn't wait that long, so we tried to rent a car. But apparently every rental car in the state was booked for the Men's College World Series baseball tournament. Our only option was to rent a U-Haul. It felt like we were in a Hollywood comedy.

Finally, we made it to Chicago and delivered the briefcase. The whole trip was a big adventure, and it was awesome to donate money to a worthwhile organization. (But take my advice: if you're looking for a comfy road trip vehicle, do *not* get a U-Haul.)

Serving others might not always be easy. But it's always worth it. In fact, it's an essential part of the Christian life. Jesus taught us to serve others, to love our neighbors as ourselves, and to put others first. He gave us many wonderful examples of how to serve, both in the way He took care of others during His life and the way He gave His life for us on the cross.

If you want to be great in God's kingdom, it starts with serving others in humility. This mentality goes against our human nature. But God is in the business of flipping the script on human expectations. Being great in God's eyes is not about being first. It's about putting others before yourself, just like Jesus did.

You don't have to take a zany cross-country trip in a U-Haul or travel on a mission trip to serve others. You can help others each day at home, school, and everywhere you go.

When you put others first, you are honoring God. That's what true greatness is all about.

— ANDREW

GOD IS IN THE BUSINESS OF FLIPPING THE SCRIPT ON HUMAN EXPECTATIONS.

OPEN EYES, OPEN HEART

> When he went ashore he saw a great crowd, and he
> had compassion on them and healed their sick.
>
> —MATTHEW 14:14

Is there ever a bad time for pizza? Here at JStu, the answer is "Definitely not!" Teenagers, in particular, have big appetites and love free food. So we set up a pizza shop inside our RV and handed out free pizza to students at a local high school.

We didn't know how many students to expect since our RV looked a bit sketchy, but people tend to gravitate toward crowds. The whole thing started with one or two kids coming over out of curiosity, and then a crowd began forming as the rumor of free pizza spread. In the end, tons of happy kids got free pizza!

If anyone knew the desires and needs of the people around Him, it was Jesus. His unique teaching and powerful miracles attracted huge crowds. In Matthew 14, the moment He stepped off a boat, hundreds—if not thousands—of people were waiting for Him.

Jesus could have walked past this throng of needy people or sent them away. After all, He was dealing with some heavy stuff of His own. He was grieving the death of His relative, John the Baptist, who had just been murdered by the king. So the last thing Jesus probably wanted to do was be around large crowds.

Nevertheless, He stopped. He had compassion on them and healed all who were sick. To Jesus, the crowd wasn't just a faceless mob. He noticed each person and had awareness of what they needed. He loved them and cared for their needs.

If we want to follow Jesus, we need to have the same attitude toward others. Our eyes should be open to the needs of those around us. No one told Justin and me the kids at that school were in desperate need of pizza. But we were high schoolers once, and we know that teens always want pizza!

Approach each day with open eyes and an open heart toward others. The more you do, the more you'll start seeing other people's needs. We all need help from time to time.

You might not give out free pizza or heal the sick. But you can make a big difference. View those around you through the eyes of Jesus, filled with compassion, love, and care. What needs do you see?

—ANDREW

APPROACH EACH DAY WITH OPEN EYES AND AN OPEN HEART TOWARD OTHERS.

GIFT GIVING

As each has received a gift, use it to serve one another, as good stewards of God's varied grace.
—1 PETER 4:10

Whether it's Christmas, your birthday, or another special occasion, it's always exciting to get gifts! But imagine if the gift you couldn't wait to open was wrapped in impenetrable layers of wood, metal, and wires. That's what we did for one of our YouTube videos, taking the anticipation of unwrapping gifts to a wild new level!

Our challenge: create an unbreakable Christmas gift, where the only way to access the goodies inside was to break in. Armed with hammers, electric drills, and saws, we embarked on a crazy quest to unlock the hidden mystery.

Starting with the worst possible tool—a rubber hammer—I faced the difficult task of breaking into this fortress of holiday packaging. As the video unfolded, we gradually unlocked better tools, making our way past multiple layers through hours of hard work and muscle strain. After an exhausting day, I finally cracked the code and reached the treasure within. (Side note: if you want to do something a little out of the ordinary this Christmas, consider an unbreakable present challenge for your family—although you might need to help Grandma with the power tools.)

We all love getting gifts, and it's even better when they don't take an entire day to open! God has given every Christian some amazing gifts that are *way* better than anything you can find under the Christmas tree. God gives each of us spiritual gifts that are tailored to our personalities and skills. Things like speaking the truth, encouraging others, teaching His Word, strong faith, and wisdom (Romans 12:3–8; 1 Corinthians 12:1–11; and 1 Peter 4:10–11). We use these gifts to glorify God, serve others, and improve our own lives. Triple-win!

You may not know what your gifts are yet, but God hasn't locked them away. He gives us free access to them, no hammers or saws required. Our gifts are naturally part of who we are, but we can learn about them and develop them by studying Scripture and putting them into practice.

When we use our talents to help others, we become living examples of Jesus to those around us. We can offer a helping hand, bring encouragement to friends and family feeling down, and inspire others to use their own gifts for God's good. So break out your spiritual gifts, and start serving others today!

— JUSTIN

SERVING OTHERS, SERVING GOD

> The King will answer them, "Truly, I say
> to you, as you did it to one of the least of
> these my brothers, you did it to me."
> —MATTHEW 25:40

For one Valentine's Day, Justin, Isaac, and I competed in a budget challenge to wow our wives with a special experience using whatever dollar amount we got on the Plinko board. I got the big-baller amount of $2,500, which (not surprisingly) I was super-stoked about. Isaac got a solid $500. And Justin? Well, he scored a whopping twenty-five bucks.

(Cue laugh track.)

I took my wife on a super-fun trip to Las Vegas. Isaac took his wife out for a really expensive meal ($230!) and some other fun activities downtown. And Justin? He made pancakes.

(Cue laugh track again.)

In all seriousness, Justin did a great job. He set a nice mood by lighting a candle and decorating their kitchen table. He made the pancake recipe his wife loves. And he also bought a thoughtful game to play with her based on something she enjoyed as a kid. All for twenty-five bucks!

Well done, partner. Well done.

No matter how big our budgets were, the goal of the video

was to serve our wives and show love to them. This sacrificial love is what Jesus asks all His followers to do. If you truly want to live for Jesus, you need to meet the needs of others, just like He did. And check this out: when you show love to others, you are showing love to Jesus Himself (Matthew 25:40)!

This world is full of selfishness. Meeting the needs of others flies in the face of this self-centered thinking. You can serve others with your time, attention, efforts, and money. And there's no end to the ways you can do it!

Don't know where to start? Check out the opportunities at your church or community center. Keep your eyes open for neighbors who could use some help. There are probably plenty of needs in your own family as well!

Remember, it isn't about how much money you spend on someone. You can show someone you care with chocolate chip pancakes just as easily as you can with a trip to Vegas. It's about putting others first with your time, thoughts, and efforts.

Jesus made His life about service. He calls you to follow His example. As you show love to others, you show love to Jesus, experience His love yourself, and point others to His love.

—ANDREW

FAMILY SERVICE PROJECT

If you are a follower of Jesus, your identity includes being a servant to others. We're called to give of ourselves for others, just as Jesus did. So here it is, the final—and perhaps most important—challenge . . .
Find somewhere meaningful to serve with your family!

IDEAS

- Plant flowers on your church property.
- Give a mom a break by babysitting.
- Gather a group of people eager to donate holiday gifts to an organization that provides presents to children in need, like Operation Christmas Child or Angel Tree.
- Write a letter to a missionary family your church supports.
- Serve a meal at a local soup kitchen.
- Help organize the closet at a local pregnancy care center.
- Collect toys to donate to a women and children's shelter.
- Volunteer to run errands for an elderly person, a person with a disability, or a refugee family.
- Collect blankets and pet food for an animal shelter.
- Pick up trash at a park or walking trail.

Justin Stuart and **Andrew Scites** are dads, friends, and creators of the popular YouTube channel **JStu**. They have a passion for creating fun content that the whole family can enjoy, and they strive to bring joy and Jesus to their young followers. The JStu motto is Laugh Daily, and the channel's purpose is to leave a positive impact on youth and encourage them to be creative and adventurous. Justin and Andrew both call Colorado Springs, Colorado, home.